Lead with Hea

Joan Marques

Lead with Heart in Mind

Treading the Noble Eightfold Path For Mindful and Sustainable Practice

Copernicus Books is a brand of Springer

Joan Marques
School of Business
Woodbury University
Burbank, CA, USA

ISBN 978-3-030-17027-1   ISBN 978-3-030-17028-8   (eBook)
https://doi.org/10.1007/978-3-030-17028-8

This Copernicus imprint is published by the registered company Springer Nature Switzerland AG
The registered company address is: Gewerbestrasse 11, 6330 Cham, Switzerland

The Majesty

Unfathomable and deceptively placid
Lies the majesty of Gaea, our planet
Source of life, precipitator of death
Vehicle, friend, foe, opportunity, and threat
Well of mystery, harbor of obscurity
Carrier of history, absorber of alleged indestructibility
Inspirator of art, instigator of fear
Humanity's undeniable frontier
Demander of reverence
Commander of existence
Oasis of time, space, dreams, and motion
The imperishable, unconquerable ocean…

~Joan Marques

We live in extraordinary times on an extraordinary planet. We encounter change at such a dazzling pace that we can barely adjust and get used to new circumstances before they disintegrate into "old news" again. And because we are creatures of habit by nature, this fast-paced trend of today's world of work and other performance areas takes a heavy toll on our sense of purpose, our level of contentment, and our general well-being.

The problems of the day are no longer far from our bed: from increased police brutality to growing minority insecurity and from escalating numbers of illegal immigrants and asylees to augmenting terrorist outbursts in unexpected corners of the world—we are affected to various degrees by these and many other turbulences. The bold statements made by the opposing candidates in the recent US presidential elections brought a number of these factors to the forefront and confronted us with multiple perspectives on these issues, some even to our utter dismay.

With growing numbers of social networks at our fingertips, our circle of concern is continuously expanding. We acquire friends in many parts of the world, and when we learn about the challenges they face, we are as concerned about them as they are about us. We also acquire insights from cultures, religions, and philosophies from outside our historical habitat and learn about behavioral ways that we never entertained as options before.

With all of the above and more happening simultaneously, we have gradually arrived at the understanding that an excessive individualistic approach toward life is no longer appropriate. In other words, we can no longer simply focus on our own progress and ignore that of others. We can no longer favor our personal bottom line over the well-being of others. Thus, we can no longer look the other way and refrain from caring about our home mates, friends, colleagues, fellow citizens, or even earthlings. The responsibility for doing the right thing has shifted from a duty of our CEOs and the government to a task that we all have to take seriously. Doing the right thing has grown out to be our common bond, and the time that any one of us could shrug and look away is over, definitely over.

This book will take the notion of a more collectivist mind-set to a level that has thus far not widely been entertained in our highly individualistic society. Tapping into Buddhism, not as a religion but more as a psychological foundation, we will discuss eight behavioral mind-sets that are essential in our decision-making processes, especially if we aspire to become more conscious and conscientious leaders to ourselves and others.

Leadership: Some Thoughts

The Optimist and the Pessimist

While part of me foresees near-future global integrations
Another part fears endless wars and hatred between nations
And while, on one hand, I truly enjoy the changing seasons
I also whine and whimper about them for millions of reasons

Some people know the art of being optimists in life:
While others have the gift to change each act into a strife
The zealots value pleasant sides of everything they see
The doomsayers make sure they never once set their minds free

Most of the time, there's part of both in every one of us
Depending on our mind-set, we accept or make a fuss
On happy days, our glass is half full, and we celebrate
In gloomy times half empty, and we cry about our fate

It brings to mind two little boys with clear opposite views
One singing morning glory, while the other cried the blues
The optimist was dancing in the fertilizing rain
The pessimist just growled out that the dancer was insane

I bet you recognize yourself in each of these two lads
The cheerful one on sunny days; the drip on days with dreads
The wisest of advises, then, may be to dance life's twist
With open heart and mind toward our inner optimist
~Joan Marques

When we compare the qualities that were considered crucial for leaders in the twentieth century with the ones that matter today, we quickly discover a world of difference. Based on a wide range of (sometimes very unpleasant and harmful) experiences, today's workforce members have arrived at some major insights. One of the most important ones is that individuals with sheer profit focus and with self-serving agendas, void of concern for the well-being of those they deal with, can no longer be considered suitable leaders. We have seen numerous companies that we once considered unbreakable sink into nothingness just like the Titanic once did. This trend turned out to be an epiphanal shift in the minds of many of us.

An interesting, but often overlooked, contributor to our changed needs and perspectives on leadership is the fact that, over the past decades, we have shifted from being an industrial economy to becoming an information society. So, while the twentieth-century economic mind-set celebrated quick financial gain, charisma, and assertiveness, today's emphasis is increasingly on integrity, communication, and flexibility.[1] Our entire idea of wealth is changing as well: from the old focus of amassing material or monetary assets to an increased appreciation of knowledge and insight—mind over matter.[2]

As practitioners and researchers of trends started looking deeper into today's preferences for leadership, a discussion emerged about the so-called "soft" and "hard" skills. Soft skills encompass behaviors of motivation, empathy, self-regulation, and social skills[3] and focus more on interpersonal relationships.[4] Hard skills pertain to intelligence, analytical/technical skills, determination, rigor, and vision and could best be classified as technical or administrative qualities that can be quantified and measured. Today's leaders should apply both, soft and hard skills, in proper balance in order to combine their astute business behavior with decent interhuman sensitivity. And so, as business leaders gain awareness of the need to combine hard and soft skills in their approaches, we are gradually entering a stage where some foundational Buddhist psychological concepts could find broad reception in contemporary workforces.

---

[1] Robles, M. M. (2012). Executive Perceptions of the Top 10 Soft Skills Needed in Today's Workplace. *Business Communication Quarterly, 75*(4), p. 453.

[2] Gilder, G. (1990). Microcosm: The Quantum Revolution in Economics and Technology. Simon and Schuster, NY.

[3] Goleman, D. (2000). Leadership that gets results. *Harvard Business Review*, March-April.

[4] Dixon, J., Belnap, C., Albrecht, C., & Lee, K. (2010). The importance of soft skills. *Corporate Finance Review, 14*(6), 35–38.

Buddhism: A Snapshot

Impermanence

Behind us
lie millions of lives -
converted to history
in fading shades of gray.
Great or unwieldy -
that no longer matters.
They led to this moment
that's now slipping away.
　　　　　　-Joan Marques

Buddhism has been around for more than 2500 years. The man we came to know as "the Buddha" was actually named Siddhartha Gautama and was the son of a tribal king. Siddhartha distanced himself from his affluent background in his 20s and acquired some valuable insights over the course of his life. These insights granted him the name of "Buddha" or the "Enlightened One."

The Buddha's insights have been passed on through the centuries and have spread worldwide. While divided in various schools or vehicles, Buddhists commonly share a number of critical foundational insights and teachings such as suffering, impermanence, no-self, karma, nirvana, dependent origination, mindfulness, the Four Noble Truths, and the Noble Eightfold Path.[5]

Buddhism aims to instill a worldview and way of living that leads to personal understanding, happiness, and wholesome development.[6] It is sometimes described as a moral, ethical, value-based, scientific, educational system, because it helps its observers to see things in their true nature, which, in turn, helps them get rid of suffering and attain happiness for themselves and others.

The foundational Buddhist thought we will use in this book is the concept of the "Four Noble Truths" which are, in fact, a sequence of insights:

1. Suffering exists
2. Suffering has a cause
3. Suffering can be ended
4. Suffering can end by observing the Noble Eightfold Path

---

[5] Marques, J. (2015). *Business and Buddhism*. Routledge. New York, NY.
[6] Johansen, B. C., & Gopalkrishna, D. (2006). A Buddhist View of Adult Learning in the Workplace. *Advances in Developing Human Resources, 8*(3), 337–345.

The Noble Eightfold Path consists of the following insights: (1) right view, (2) right intention, (3) right speech, (4) right action, (5) right livelihood, (6) right effort, (7) right mindfulness, and (8) right concentration. There is no specific sequence in these insights, because they are interrelated.

In this book, we plan to devote a chapter to each element of the eightfold path, thus bringing that specific element within the scope of leadership. In order to establish a link with today's leaders and enhance readers' understanding, examples of today's leaders will be reviewed. Please see the brief Table of Contents in the next pages for a clearer overview.

Contributions of this Book to the Leadership Field

While Buddhism has been brought within the scope of leadership before, there has not been any book in which the eightfold path has been explicitly presented as an instrument toward more responsible, future-oriented leadership. This book aims to explain the workings of the eightfold path by demonstrating the interdependency of all its elements: there is no right intention without right view, there is no right speech without right intention, there is no right action without right speech, etc. This also implies that the leaders to be presented in this work could be placed at any element of the path and still be reviewed in a sensible way.

By presenting the elements of the eightfold path as a personal and/or professional leadership practice, the book questions the excessive bottom-line focus and the hard-nosed approach that has been part of the so-called leadership practices in recent decades. While the notion of applying the ancient noble eightfold path as a leadership tool for today and tomorrow may seem idealistic, readers will find that all of the leaders we discuss as practitioners of the eightfold path are very realistic in their approach and have thus far gained much honor, attention, and acclaim through practices that were once considered too idealistic.

Contents

1

What's Going On with Leadership?

One Moment

In this one-moment breathe
I share a one-moment poem
With some one-moment lines
For you

About this one-moment life that,
After one-moment struggles
And a one-moment glory,
Is through

We make one-moment fuss
Of a one-moment loss
And feel one-moment pride
For a one-moment stride

But this one-moment came
And the moment will go
And tomorrow we're all…
Well, you know…

~Joan Marques

A couple of days before I started writing this chapter, I saw a note from Nina on my Facebook wall. Nina used to be one of my MBA students several years ago and started out as a bright and zesty participant. Nina was going to conquer the world! She was witty, smart, and fun-loving. Then, something

© Springer Nature Switzerland AG 2019
J. Marques, *Lead with Heart in Mind*, https://doi.org/10.1007/978-3-030-17028-8_1

changed. Her participation diminished, the quality of her work decreased, and most of the time, she stared into the room with a far-away look. I wasn't sure if I should approach her, since she was still doing reasonably well, according to general standards. I just knew instinctively, however, that this was not all Nina could be.

Fortunately, I didn't have to ask. One evening, Nina asked me to step outside with her, and she broke down. It was like standing under the Niagara Falls! She let it all out: she had been in a bad relationship for quite some time and couldn't find a way to properly end it. Her partner was on drugs and mentally unstable, and she wanted to move on: make something of her life. She had started to realize that this wasn't the way she would make it, though. Yet, while she wanted to choose for herself, she was also terrified that merely turning away from her weak partner, whom she had known for many years, might lead him to do something she would not forgive herself for, like regressing even further into his drug usage or simply committing suicide.

It was a long talk, and I had to step outside my own mental and emotional boundaries to reach out to this desperate soul that had so much potential. Somehow, I must have managed to succeed, because Nina bounced back after that conversation, rediscovered her bubbly self, took leadership of her life, and graduated at the top of her class. Today, she is a promising music producer, and her Facebook note revealed that she did not forget our critical conversation. What I remember best from that conversation is that I had to search deep inside myself to find those words that would give Nina the support and believe in herself and help her overcome the sense of guilt that kept her in such a hopeless situation.

In my opinion, that's what leadership is about today: breaking through our own barriers in order to dig out qualities that we know reside in others, thus assisting them in becoming the best they can be. There are no guidelines for leading others, and in fact, there are no set theories either. Today, nothing less than a rich combination of several leadership tactics will work. People are, on average, better educated than before in many parts of the world. They are also better connected and informed. Many of us use the Internet and a range of social media every day, so we learn about other practices and can measure our own circumstances to those.

Leading people has not always been practiced that way, however, and it's still not practiced that way everywhere. Just a century ago, leadership was oftentimes a matter of giving orders and keeping track if they were followed well. Lots of workplaces were family-owned, so the quality of the leader you got in such workplaces depended on how lucky you were. There could be a compassionate founder-leader, like Sam Walton, who would do his best to make his employees experience a family atmosphere and feel content in their workplace, but then there could be a next generation of leaders, just like the successors of Sam Walton, who are entirely disconnected and uncaring about the wellness of any type of stakeholder—neither their manufacturers nor their salesforce—because they only care about enlarging their bank accounts.

Yet, there is a promising trend happening: the leaders we'll see in future years will be shaped by the wishes of those who *want* to be led by them. The dynamics will shift, and employees will increasingly dictate the qualities and behavior they desire from their leaders.

The Role of Business

Inner Dialogue

Hello, my peaceful right hemisphere,
I've come to visit you again, my dear
After a day of measuring in endless trance
Ensuring ongoing improvement and excellence
Progress, competition, and the bottom-line
I can feel the stress running up my spine

Here's a world where all that may count
Is whether our annual reports are sound
Where, in spite of all the media, no one sees
The suffering of humans, animals, and trees
Instead of addressing those troubles today
We simply prefer to measure all the way

We've elevated the frivolous to a serious trend
And reduced the serious to almost non-existent
We are changing many things – year after year
But not all for wellness of the living, I fear
We rather focus on a haughty performance ride
While inner-peace is on a downward slide
                                    -Joan Marques

Business is often credited with bringing change, growth, and development, but we should consider that these trends can have positive or negative effects on a society. Indeed, business can enter where others cannot. Even though people are aware that business corporations can affect their environment in positive as well as negative ways, they usually embrace these corporations, simply because corporations create employment and other opportunities. Indeed, whatever a company's intentions really are, the fact that it operates in your city, state, or country, leads to activity, and oftentimes creates a snowball effect in that it encourages other businesses to follow. So, development is an almost logical consequence of a business establishment, even if that may not be the business organizations' primary focus.

The Good Side

As indicated above, business corporations often bring progress in communities, whether that is their intention or not. They build factories and offices and bring employment opportunities by hiring local workers and often also by using the services of local distribution networks; and they most likely purchase as many local resources as possible, if only to reduce costs. Then there are the taxes that such corporations have to pay to the local government, and the infrastructure they have to develop or improve when starting or expanding their operations. And not to forget, there are the other organizations, suppliers, competitors, or complementary product creators that usually follow the first movers.

All of these factors bring development into a location, in the short term, and oftentimes also in the long term. Over time, living standards may start rising, and locals may get encouraged to start their own entrepreneurial venues in which they may develop spinoffs or come up with revolutionary alternatives. Depending on the location, a corporation may also bring development for the community as a whole, for instance, through increased living standards, through the increased choices it offers, through its influence on the local education system, and by encouraging people to rethink outdated and sometimes useless habits through cultural influence. Gradually, an entire society can change, thanks to the establishment of one business corporation, which caused a snowball effect in positive sense.

The Bad Side

There is no good without bad. Some people even say that we need the bad to continue appreciating the good. Yet, some bad developments are of so enormous that recovery from them is almost impossible or happens extremely slow. The first negative effect from business entities in any location is the waste, especially the industrial waste. Pollution, exhaustion of natural resources, abuse of local workers, and using local grounds as major dumping areas are only some of the disastrous effects that business corporations can bring along.

Many of these behaviors happen till today by business organizations that should know better, but choose to use double standards in their operations. This is why we sometimes see the same company that performs like a role model in the USA or Western Europe takes grave advantage of people in some South American, African, or Asian countries. This, then, illustrates that change, growth, and development are not always beneficial to local communities.

Some types of change can bring more setbacks than advancement, for instance, when people who used to live peacefully together in a village now become each other's archenemies, simply due to the establishment of a corporation, which may cause some to benefit more than others. An example is the ethnic conflict in the Niger Delta,[1] which arose in the early 1990s as a result of tensions between foreign oil corporations (Shell and Chevron) and some Niger Delta minority ethnic groups. The fact that these local groups, particularly the Ogoni and the Ijaw, felt exploited created an unhealthy climate of ethnic and political unrest, which was still going on at the time this book was written. The fierce competition for oil wealth, which was the foundation of this friction, gave rise to such violence between ethnic groups that the entire region had to be militarized. The earlier mentioned civil unrest in the Niger Delta may serve as a good example that some types of growth should be curtailed. The powerful multinational corporations have become closely involved in the military's actions to manhandle, and even kill, local people who have the nerve to protest at the hazards caused by the oil companies.[2]

There are other ways in which industrial growth should be curtailed. For instance, when it pertains to the growth of people with asthma, or cancer, due to industrial vapors, or when genetically modified crops are brought to areas where health conscious, natural trends were maintained for the longest time. Some older readers may remember the asbestos case that has led to numerous litigations in the twentieth century. Asbestos is a mineral substance that was used for several purposes but most dominantly as electrical insulation for hotplate wiring and for building insulation. The most prominent asbestos-producing company in the USA was the Johns Manville Corporation. Even

---

[1] Hook, J. & Ganguly, R. (2000). Multinational Corporations and Ethnic Conflict: Theory and Experience, *Nationalism and Ethnic Politics* 6(1), 48–71.

[2] Shah, A. (2002). Corporate interests and actions can harm the environment. *Global Issues: Social, Political, Economic and Environmental Issues That Affect Us All*. Retrieved on 11 October 2013 from http://www.globalissues.org/article/55/corporations-and-the-environment#Corporateinterestsandaction scanharmtheenvironment

though evidence about the health issues related to asbestos surfaced as early as 1918,[3] it took decades before authorities openly admitted that asbestos was a health hazard and that it could lead to asbestosis, lung cancer, and malignant mesothelioma. With the destructive effects finally in the open, the Johns Manville Corporation faced thousands of lawsuits between 1960 and 1990, and this huge corporation filed for chapter 11 bankruptcy protection in 1982. In 1988 the company emerged from the protection and is still flourishing today.

Some developments may bring more destruction than advancement, such as factories that produce such toxic waste that entire communities start suffering from the results of their performance. A classic example is corporate giant Monsanto's decade long dumping of highly toxic PCBs in Anniston, Alabama.[4] For almost 40 years, Monsanto discharged its toxic waste from industrial coolants into a creek in Anniston. As it turns out, Monsanto executives knew since the mid-1960s that fish in that creek were dying within 10 seconds due to the extreme toxicity of their waste dumps, but they decided to keep the information hidden. The local population was literally dirt poor, so no one was too concerned. When the unethical, repulsive acts of Monsanto were exposed, the company invested only $40 million in cleanup practices and granted about $80 million in legal settlements.[5]

The Reputation of Business

The factors above demonstrate why business, as a whole, is often accused of smothering local trends, disrupting local economies, depleting resources, and tarnishing cultural values. Admitted, some leaders are trying to increase socially responsible performance within their companies, but unfortunately, many others still blatantly continue with destructive processes. In many countries and states, it is still cheaper to react to environmental policies than to proactively do the right thing. In other words, corporations are well-aware that a penalty for toxic waste will cost them only a fraction of what they would pay to reduce their toxic waste overall. As a result, the company's leaders decide to continue behaving irresponsibly until the company gets fined. History has presented us many of these cases, especially in the oil industry, where the fine for an oil spill or explosion due to insufficient safety measures

---

[3] A History of the Deadly Dust. (2000). *Multinational Monitor, 21*(9), 20.
[4] Grunwald, M. (Jan. 1, 2002). Monsanto Hid Decades Of Pollution PCBs Drenched Ala. Town, But No One Was Ever Told. *The Washington Post*. Retrieved on October 11 2013 from http://www.commondreams.org/headlines02/0101-02.htm
[5] Ibid.

does not even amount to a month's revenue for that company. On top of that, many of these corporations know that they can appeal their fines and then end up paying even less than the initial penalty. In the end, they stretch the payment of their fine over a long period of time, so they barely experience any hardship that way.

What People Want from Their Leaders Today

As I was having lunch with Juillet, one of my former MBA students, in the well-attended, fairly large restaurant across the campus, our orders were delivered by a kind gentleman, named Charbel. When Charbel saw me sitting, a broad smile broke through his face, and he greeted me enthusiastically. As he walked off, I told Juillet that Charbel was also an alumnus from the program. She looked puzzled and said, "So, what is he doing here serving customers then?" I proudly smiled and said, "He owns the place."

I was particularly proud of pointing out Charbel's serving of the meals, as it underscored to me how engaged his leadership style really was: he participated in every part of the restaurant's practices, from negotiating with suppliers and hiring employees to assisting in the kitchen and serving the food. Charbel loved the contacts he established with customers and felt that he learned more than anyone could tell him from his personal interactions with the customer. Over the years since Charbel had graduated, he has become a regular guest speaker on entrepreneurship and engaged leadership in my classes, because he literally lives these practices on a daily basis and understands that it makes all the difference.

Employees in today's workplaces are very clear and forthright in their ideas about leadership. If we compare the qualities that were considered important for leaders in the twentieth century with the ones that matter most now, we discover a world of difference. There are many reasons that led to this shift, but one of the most important ones is experience. In the first decade of the twenty-first century, particularly, it became obvious that the old ideas about what leaders should be like led to disastrous outcomes. The old but still infamous cases of Enron, Tyco, WorldCom, and Arthur Andersen speak volumes: all these corporations were led by people who were smart, assertive, extroverted, and charismatic, but not very concerned with the well-being of their employees and the communities they served. In fact, these leaders were so focused on the bottom line, that they took the worst advantage possible of society, and left many stakeholders in grueling economic hardship once they got caught and lost their positions.

Fortunately, there is rarely a bad experience that in the end does not lead to something good. What has emerged from the rubbles of these devastating corporate demises is an elevation of employees' awareness. More and more working people have started wondering why some skills used to be shunned from workplaces and whether it's not time to reevaluate the behavioral traits leaders should nurture in order to keep their workplaces afloat while, at the same time, ensuring employee satisfaction.

It became increasingly clear that the Industrial Revolution had run its course and that we have collectively moved into a Knowledge Revolution, which requires an entirely different construction in workplace dynamics. Values such as integrity, communication, and flexibility[6] have gained immense popularity among the working class. The entire concept of "wealth" has changed: no longer is it seen as an accrual of material or monetary assets. Instead, the wealth of knowledge and understanding has risen to the forefront.[7] Even if we cannot see this trend as clearly in all work environments as we would wish, it remains a fact that the exchange of intellectual output is rapidly surpassing the exchange of goods and services in importance.[8] As this trend keeps growing, employees keep calling for a more balanced set of skills in their leaders.

Leadership and Wakefulness

Wakefulness has yet to be widely established as a leadership style, but once fully understood and evaluated on its many advantages for leaders, their followers, and their organizations, it will get there. Let's look at the concept of wakefulness as a leadership skill; examine some of the rewards for leaders and their organizations of applying awakened leadership; and consider some of the disadvantages of not applying awakened leadership.

Wakefulness, although practiced by various leaders, has thus far not been formally identified as a specific leadership trait. Yet if you look deeper, you may find that some leaders are applying wakefulness, sometimes partially and sometimes fully. Awakened leaders maintain a high level of alertness in every regard: toward themselves and their driving motives in various matters, toward the people and organizations they lead, toward the environment in which their organizations operate, and toward the entire universe. In more popular

---

[6] Robles, M. M. (2012). Executive Perceptions of the Top 10 Soft Skills Needed in Today's Workplace. *Business Communication Quarterly, 75*(4), p. 453.

[7] Gilder, G. (1990). Microcosm: The Quantum Revolution in Economics and Technology. Simon and Schuster, NY.

[8] Rifkin, J. (2000). *The Age of Access*. Penguin Putnam, New York.

terms, an awakened leader could be described as a "situational-plus" leader. A situational leader is one who modifies his or her leadership style on the basis of both the situation and the people he or she works with. Such leaders evaluate these two factors and then determine the leadership style that will work best under the circumstances. Awakened leadership goes far beyond situational leadership, however. The wakeful leader also pays close attention to the organization's mission and the well-being of all stakeholders. This means that an awakened leader practices the elements of the Noble Eightfold Path (to be discussed in this book) and therefore remains aware of environmental issues, societal issues, and the interests of customers, suppliers, and other constituents before determining his or her leadership style.

Four Approaches

The wakeful aspect of leading is initially difficult to understand but is easy to apply once mastered. The awakened leader first decides whether to take a task and/or a relationship orientation to the issue at hand (i.e., he or she chooses between the two main areas of leading) and then determines which of four approaches to leadership—laissez-faire, empathetic, autocratic, or democratic (which together form the acronym LEAD)—will work best.

- The laissez-faire approach works best in organizations that have a strong sense of self-direction—such as law firms, consultancies, and high-tech companies—and in which every worker is highly skilled and manages his or her own circle of clients.
- The empathetic approach works best in organizations that are fairly small and primarily people oriented. Many nonprofit organizations fit into this category.
- The autocratic approach is not the most popular style, but there are organizations in which it works. For example, it is useful when a crisis occurs, and the leader is expected to give directions instead of calling a meeting and finding out what everyone suggests. The armed forces, because they often have to act on the spur of the moment and in crisis situations, are receptive to this leadership style.
- The democratic approach, in which meetings are usually held to share information about emerging issues and to contemplate possible solutions, lends itself especially well to the academic environment. But determining whether to take a people or a process approach and subsequently deepening one's choice by reviewing the four styles are just half the work of implementing awakened leadership.

The next step for the leader is to evaluate, and if possible develop, a set of traits that will support a wakeful approach. Emotional intelligence and authenticity are the major requirements here. Emotional intelligence is important because the awakened leader needs to know where he or she comes from, to be in touch with his or her values and morals, and to be attuned to co-workers' values and morals. Authenticity is important because people are finally starting to realize that it is unnatural to park one's soul at the door when entering the workplace. Bringing your entire self into the workplace, without fear of being ridiculed or backstabbed, and using your entire self for the betterment of yourself and your organization are the keys to authenticity.

Face The Music

There are numerous consequences of not being wakeful. Leaders who refrain from a wakeful approach in today's increasingly interdependent business world will find themselves becoming outsiders in the global village. The continuous intermingling of cultures leaves no room for holding onto a single leadership style. Even when a leader operates in just one city, county, or state, he or she will find the need to apply an awakened approach because workforces are becoming more multiethnic and multicultural and display an increasing diversity of ages and skills.

Organizations in which leaders employ a single style—even if this style has worked well in the past—will find themselves at a disadvantage compared with competitors who move faster because they have mastered the multidimensional approach of wakefulness. Organizations with wakeful leaders are more open to change and therefore encourage organizational learning, both inside and outside the work environments. These organizations encourage workers to continuously question current processes in the workplace and to suggest improved methods. They focus on encouraging continuous education among their workers, realizing that even though some workers may exit once they have obtained an increased level of skills and knowledge, workers who feel valued and encouraged are less likely to leave a nurturing environment. This decreases turnover and enhances the organization's quality of output, which in turn positively affects the bottom line.

Words of Wisdom

I asked a number of leaders that I considered wakeful in their approaches, what advice they had for leaders who are aspiring to become more wakeful, and they suggested the following:

- See your responsibility in a much broader way. Too many business executives are overly occupied with a narrow vision and don't consider the full responsibilities their companies have to the societies in which they operate. It is important that today's leaders consider their responsibilities beyond the bottom line.
- Walk your talk. Pay more than lip service to your relationships with your employees. Mission statements should be more than just plaques on walls or desks. One leader said, "If you take good care of your people, they will take good care of you and your mission."
- Be more in touch with all levels of your company. Encourage a team spirit and an elevated sense of meaning. This will lead to greater employee satisfaction and, ultimately, increased productivity.
- Promote a corporate culture that addresses humanity as a whole. Focus on all stakeholders (workers, shareholders, customers, suppliers, and society) rather than just the stockholders.
- Continue to develop the qualities of awakened leadership. By doing so, you will convert leadership from a duty to a highly gratifying experience.

Awakened Leadership: A Behavioral Roadmap

As you may have gathered thus far, awakened leadership could be labeled as one of several "new-age" leadership styles, born out of frustration with the self-centered, greed-based, mindless leadership actions of past decades, or it can be considered an entire way of being.

Regardless of how you decide to look at it, it remains a highly useful way of dealing with the responsibility of leadership in any setting, whether private or professional; small, mid-sized, or large scaled; or pertaining to the self or others.

So, what is so useful about it? The main reason is this: Awakened leadership is reflective. When you reflect on things, you consider them from multiple angles and think deeper about them than a superficial thought or two. Your job, position, and work relationships, the industry you are involved in, the very purpose of your performance, your private or social connections, the things you say, the things you do, and those you refrain from saying and doing: reflecting on all of the above can help you understand yourself better and make you more mindful from here onward.

One of the greatest favors you can do yourself is understanding why you do what you do and who is affected by your actions. Especially when you are about to make major decisions, such as laying off a number of employees, discontinuing or starting a new production or service line, engaging in a new relationship, or terminating an old one, it may be helpful if you write down the perceived impact. When considering important steps, we often underestimate the number of stakeholders whose lives will be influenced by these steps. Take a few minutes and start writing. The group of affected parties is usually five times higher than what your initial thoughts may have wanted you to believe.

Awakened leadership is the opposite of sleepwalking leadership. First: what is sleepwalking leadership? It is the trend of making decisions without considering that:

1. Everything changes, and nothing is today as it was yesterday, so you cannot continue to make the same decisions you made yesterday hoping they will have the same outcomes.
2. "Reality," as you see it, is not the same as how others see it. Your reality is shaped by a number of influencing factors, such as your upbringing, culture, character, generation, education, values, and more. You can therefore not consider that others will always understand and appreciate your perspectives.
3. Traditional patterns or habits are the most common ways of driving you into the autopilot state, thus sleepwalking mode: you follow these patterns or apply these habits without thinking and, definitely, without reflecting if they still make sense in your life as it is today. Mindlessly submitting to recurring patterns or habits makes us followers, not leaders.
4. Focusing too much on the details can make you lose sight of the bigger purpose of something. Some people can get so lost in the details that these become the main goal of their performance, causing them to entirely lose track of the larger scheme of things.
5. Mindless leadership has maneuvered us into a global ecological crisis, and every plan, step, decision, or action you undertake from now on—individually or collectively—will either be instrumental to a positive turnaround or will further augment the problems we, the human species, have created in the past century.

With the above stipulated, awakened leadership can easily be understood, through the following behavioral roadmap. Awakened leadership is the continued awareness in your thoughts, actions, and communications that:

1. You have to make your decisions by reflecting on your lessons learned from past experiences, but even more by reflection on your wishes for the future and the possible effects these decisions will have on that.
2. You should consider the perspectives of others and keep an open mind to potentially different ideas, as they may enrich your understanding, insight, and, consequently, the directions you will choose going forward.
3. You should question, even doubt, established patterns and procedures, as many of them were created when times, expectations, circumstances, goals, and mindsets were entirely different. If you find that the old patterns and procedures still suffice, you can continue with them, but if you find that there is room for improvement or drastic change, you should implement that.
4. You should keep in mind that while details are important to safeguard quality in everything, you also have to keep the big picture in mind, so that you can focus on what really matters in the long run.
5. You should make mindful leadership your new habit. Your mind is a wonderful instrument, but it has the tendency to lead you astray at every opportunity it gets. This is the time to step up in awareness and regain control over the directions your mind moves into.

Restore your priorities in the right order, and realize the impermanence of everything, including yourself. If you can keep yourself mindful of the fact that you want to leave this world a better place than you encountered it, you have set an important step on the path to awakened leadership.

Marc Benioff and Salesforce

A good example of the kind of leader today's generation of workers seem to call for is Marc Benioff, founder and CEO of Salesforce, an Internet company with about 28,000 employees, that ranked no 1 on Fortune's 2017 Future 50 leaders list of companies with a market value above $20 billion that are exceptional and should be followed. Innovation and creativity seem to be the fluid that streams through Benioff's veins. Salesforce's product line is not so much revolutionary in our times, as is its entire approach to business. Benioff's company is known for three business trends that are now established in daily performance or have been adopted by many business people: (1) a technology model now known as the cloud, (2) the subscription business model, and (3) the 1-1-1 model, the latter being Salesforce's philanthropic commitment to give away 1% each of equity, products, and employee hours.

One of the main reasons to conclude that Benioff must be doing something good is the fact that his strategies have been widely copied by more than 3000 current business leaders. It seems that leading business assessment authorities such as Wall Street have their eyes on Salesforce as an auspicious trendsetter, not merely through its own growth but also through well-considered acquisitions. In the past decade alone, Salesforce has acquired 55 companies, which manifested innovativeness or market pioneering. Yet, what makes Salesforce—and Benioff—so special is their approach to giving: social causes such as funding of schools, hospitals, and other well-being-focused entities receive millions of dollars in support from Salesforce.

In 2018 Benioff was the sole billionaire supporter of a San Francisco ballot measure addressing homelessness ("Prop C"), which turned into a national "Battle of the Big-Tech Titans." Prop C, which ultimately passed with 60% of votes, aims to raise an additional $250–$300 million in corporate taxes annually—making it the largest tax increase in city history—for a fund dedicated to solving the homeless crisis in San Francisco. The companies with the highest revenues will have to pay the most to support this effort. What made Prop C such a hot topic was the fact that it started as a grassroots voter initiative, but became an elite political battleground as soon as it got elevated into a Twitter debate between billionaires.

Several billionaires expressed their opposition against Prop C, claiming that they did not consider it the proper way to help the homeless community. Even the San Francisco mayor at the time, London Breed, opposed the proposition and listed a number of reasons why he felt Prop C should not be supported. One of those reasons was that there had already been $300 million spent on homeless programs and that businesses might leave San Francisco with such a high tax to pay for homeless support.[9]

Considering the Prop C homeless tax in hindsight, Benioff stated that he had priests, rabbis, and imams helping him, but no other CEOs. It was only after Prop C won the popular vote that other business leaders finally started dripping in with their support pledges. Benioff holds the opinion that many of these late CEO supporters have decided to make a support pledge after their employees expressed disappointment in these leaders' callous ignorance of the homelessness problem.[10]

---

[9] Au-Yeung, A. (2018). San Francisco Voters Approve Tax Ballot Measure To Help Homeless, Tech Billionaire Marc Benioff Wins Big. *Forbes.Com*, 4.

[10] Ghaffary, S. (14 Nov, 2018). Marc Benioff says he had rabbis and imams supporting the Prop C homelessness tax—but not tech CEOs. *Recode*. Retrieved from https://www.recode.net/2018/11/14/18093170/marc-benioff-homeless-tax-prop-c-tech-ceos

As for the way Salesforce is conducting its business practice, the entire product and service package the company offers is geared toward ease, affordability, and timeliness. By putting its products online, the company ensures that customers always have access to the latest version of the software they use without frustration, delay, or extra expenses. Benioff has adopted and performs with the understanding that business success should not only be focused on shareholders but that all stakeholders should benefit. Employees are encouraged to use the "Ohana" (family) floor that is included in each Salesforce building. The Ohana floor is a community space where all employees are welcome to share in the family atmosphere.[11]

Benioff is very much invested in Salesforce, but doesn't plan to keep the company at all costs. He admits that doing a good job as a leader takes about 95% of one's time and that there is more to life than working all the time. So far, however, he stays at the helm and continues to set revolutionary, yet humane trends in his leadership and corporate performance.

Counting Blessings

I was about to count my blessings
I thought it would be time well-spent
But soon found out that I didn't know
Where to start or where to end

Every day brings me so many
Starting with being able to rise
Ending with a bed to sleep in
And in-between just endless supplies…

My work, my family, and my children
My grandkids and my living space
My darling pets, who teach me kindness
My health, which I so much embrace

Experiences I sometimes dreaded
But that now help me see things clear
Awareness that just keeps expanding
Accepting all that lives as dear

---

[11] Lashinsky, A. (2017). Benioff in Bloom. (cover story). *Fortune, 176*(6), 64–72.

At last, I stopped my counting efforts
So many blessings, just for me
But it was good to take a moment
To think on them and clearly see

That the act of counting blessings
Is simply an ungrateful way
To value an infinite supply
I take for granted every day

2

How Buddhist Thinking Fits in Leadership

Not sure…

It seems that most people
Need to hear some kind of sound
Which means that, in most places,
There's no quietude to be found

In absence of media, phone or friend,
Many prefer to hear their own voice
Consumed by this ceaseless craving
For any kind of conceivable noise

Perhaps silence is now taboo
This jewel of a substance so fine
This soothing mental blanket
Frail sanctuary – sacred shrine

Oasis of listening to thoughts
Honoring the breath given at birth
Reacquainting with forgotten senses
And savoring the stillness of Earth

Why is silence so hard to find?
Are most thoughts too hard to endure?
Why do people ignore their mind?
I'm at a loss here… I'm not sure.

–Joan Marques

© Springer Nature Switzerland AG 2019
J. Marques, *Lead with Heart in Mind*, https://doi.org/10.1007/978-3-030-17028-8_2

Buddhism is sometimes considered a religion, but increasingly, people realize that Buddhist practices don't necessarily have to infringe with their religious views and values. Buddhism can very well be considered a way of living. Buddhism is summarized reference to the teachings of the Buddha. A Buddha is a person who attained Bodhi, which means wisdom in meaningful, morally responsible thinking and behaving. "Buddha" therefore means "enlightened one." The first person to be generally known as "Buddha," and also the one credited as the founder of Buddhism, was Siddhartha Gautama, the son of an Indian tribal leader. While Siddhartha enjoyed the privileges of his life at a young age, his confrontation with sickness, old age, and death as a young adult made him realize that life was not always a bed of roses. He promptly left his privileged life behind and set out to seek wisdom, which he obtained in his mid-30s after much wandering and many struggles.

Siddhartha engaged in insight meditation, also known as "Vipassana," and so gained insight in the fact that everything is interdependent and everything is impermanent: nothing lasts. The fact that he referred to himself as "awake" afterward got him the name "Buddha." Over the next 45 years, the Buddha listened to many people and shared many insights, with the Four Noble Truths, including the Noble Eightfold Path, as some of the key concepts.

The Four Noble Truths

The Four Noble Truths reflect life at its core. In the most basic terms, they are as follows:

1. Suffering exists.
2. Suffering has a cause.
3. Suffering can be ended.
4. There is a path to end suffering, which is the Noble Eightfold Path.

The first three Noble Truths are intended to enhance our understanding about the need and purpose of the Noble Eightfold Path.

The Noble Eightfold Path comprises eight interrelated practices: right view, right intention, right speech, right action, right livelihood, right effort, right mindfulness, and right concentration. The practices are not numbered, because they should not be seen as a sequence with any specific order, but rather as a set of practices that are incomplete without each other.

It may be useful to elaborate slightly on each of the above concepts to help us obtain a better understanding of them.

The First Noble Truth tells us that suffering exists. Suffering should be seen in a much broader context here than a specific pain or ailment. The context that the Buddha used here was that life in general brings many forms of suffering along: birth, aging, illness, death, sad and disheartening experiences, the loss of something or someone precious, the inability to get something or someone we want, and more. Even if we would say that many of these moments can be seen as highlights, there is still always an element of suffering involved.

Let's dwell on some examples: birth is considered a beautiful process, but it's also a fact that most women endure tremendous labor pains and most babies cry at birth, as they are being released from the warm, comfortable home that is their mother's womb. Therefore, babies need warmth and loving care to gain trust in the unknown, noisy world in which they land. Unfortunately, many children don't experience this warmth, as some are unwanted, and others are born prematurely or with a condition that may require them to be secluded from the warmth of their parents for quite some time. Birth can bring suffering in many other ways in today's society: first of all, we're dealing with global overpopulation whereby there are still more births than deaths in the world. In fact, in 2017 alone, there were about 2.5 times more births than deaths globally, pushing the global population up to almost 7.6 billion. As the global population keeps growing, the need for food increases, and resources become scarcer. About every 10 seconds, a person dies of hunger in the world. The largest of these hunger deaths are among children. As you can gather, there is much to be considered when we are thinking of birth, because the world is a very interconnected place, and every action affects another in ways we cannot even begin to imagine.

Aging is often considered a blessing, but many aging people will tell you about the problems they experience with loss of mobility, dulled senses (loss of hearing, smelling, or tasting), and a loss of zest for new experiences. A majority of aging people acquire a greater appreciation for their home environment and find it hard to uproot themselves, even if only for a work- or vacation-based trip. Many of them consider a long drive, a busy airport, a plane flight, staying in a hotel, and spending time among unknown people in unknown places rather stressful. Engaging in the demands of life can therefore bring mental and physical suffering to those aging people who would prefer to stay in their comfort zones.

Illness, by default, implicates suffering, but in that suffering, we can identify various degrees, depending on the type of illness and the way an ill person feels about it. Some people have an exceptional ability of making their illness an enriching experience to others. Randy Pausch, for instance, was a brilliant researcher and pioneering educator, who was diagnosed with pancreatic cancer and knew he was dying. Shortly after learning about his inevitable fate, he organized an inspirational "last lecture" in Carnegie Mellon, in which he reflected on achieving his childhood dreams. This lecture is reviewed by millions till today. Yet, regardless of the noble and courageous, insightful contribution, Pausch suffered from the awareness that he would not see his three lovely children grow up to become adults. His children also suffered because they had to grow up without this inspirational force in their lives.

As for death, the first form of suffering that comes to mind is the awareness we all have that we will die someday and have no prior knowledge of when that day will be and how death will come upon us. While some people prepare themselves spiritually for their transition from this stage to the next, there is a mystique captured in death that we experience in different ways at different times. Death can also bring suffering when it pertains to a beloved person or pet, who passes before us. Even though that person or pet may be relieved from pain and sorrow by dying, those of us who stay behind suffer from missing this loved one and may do so for a long time.

Sad and disheartening situations also bring suffering. Death and illness are just some of these experiences, but life presents us with so much more: losing a job; losing a home; having to move and leave a familiar place behind; experiencing the departure of beloved family members, friends, or colleagues; going through a break up or a divorce; or yearning for a special someone who is not interested in us or is devoted to another—there are numerous small, medium, and large experiences that bring about some sort of suffering. In California, where I live, there are several wildfires every year. Around the time of writing this chapter, there were four major wildfires running simultaneously in Southern California, with one, the Thomas fire, burning for over a month and demolishing more than 1000 structures. Among these structures were homes from people who had made plans to live long and happily in their dwellings, yet found themselves homeless from one day to another. Some people lost their pets in the process of a rushed evacuation. These surprises of life can be very depressing and cause a lot of emotional, physical, and financial suffering to those involved.

Now, the above enumeration can make you think that life is an unending sequence of suffering, but that would not be a healthy and uplifting way to look at it. In saying that suffering exists, it was not the Buddha's intention to make life seem as a sequence of miseries, but, rather, to make us aware of the basics of existence. It's simple and true: we all have to deal with suffering, and we do so at many stages in our lives. Just think about it: life can feel beautiful and rosy at any given moment, but there is always something that could be better. Our lives always have some imperfections, and even if we achieved the most desirable state, we find that there is always just one more thing left to be desired. Studies have found that even people who win the lottery and become multimillionaires get used to their new situation and resume their initial mental state once the initial high has subsided. After all, money cannot buy us everything, so if there are ailments, losses of dear ones, or some state of depression, wealth will not be able to turn the tide. This goes to show that even when we think we have achieved our dearest goals, life continues to happen, and we will encounter a new set of pleasant and unpleasant surprises, some of which will elate us and others, which will bring suffering.

The Second Noble Truth implies that suffering has a cause. In the explanations above, I have amply explained the causes of suffering. Some of these causes are external and cannot be avoided, such as death of a loved one or losing our job. Yet, there are other causes of suffering that we can address internally. Sometimes we suffer because we are envious of someone else's performance and mirror that to our own. Comparing is a strong cause of suffering. Yet, it's avoidable. If you can train yourself to stop comparing, the cause of that suffering is gone.

Very often, we also bring suffering upon ourselves by craving something we don't have. We have the power to instill in our mind what we do and don't need, and so, we can mentally escalate things into obsessions when there is really no need to. Think of the annual race to get a new iPhone, for instance. Many people feel that if they have not purchased the latest model of this device, they might be seen as unable to keep up with today's trend. And even if their "old" phone works perfectly fine, they will do anything in their power—even get themselves into debt—to get the newest phone. Much of this type of suffering, believe it or not, we bring upon ourselves. If our friends judge us on basis of the newness of our mobile phone, computer, outfit, car, or other gimmick, they are not really friends in the first place. Maneuvering yourself in trouble only to get something that you really can't afford is a powerful cause of suffering today.

Sadly, many people engage in this behavior: they judge others on the newness or perceived expensiveness of their clothes, shoes, cars, phones, or even the house and neighborhood they live in. This means that many people then become victims of this trend, because they don't want to be seen as "obsolete" or "unable to step up."

Another cause of suffering is the dissatisfaction that so many of us have acquired about the way we look. The media bombard us every day with images of how we should look ideally. The concepts of "beauty" and "handsomeness" have been molded in a certain format, so those who don't match this mold may become very dissatisfied, even disheartened, due to the perception that was instilled into them that they don't meet the standards of desirableness. This problem is particularly painful in young people, teenagers, because they are still very sensitive to the influences of their environment. However, there are also more seasoned people who remain influenced by trends of which they feel they should be a part.

Fortunately, we can do something about these forms of suffering. The first step toward ending this type of suffering is awareness, which will be discussed in the next Noble Truth. Yet, before we get there, we should also consider the following: in our lifetime we change continuously. At every stage, there are some things we gain and some things we lose. Once we attain the things we desire, we move on, and new areas of desire emerge. Think of this familiar example: you graduate and desire to get a job, so you can earn your own money. So you suffer through many searches, applications, and interviews, until you find a job. Then, you may realize that this job is really not what you want to do for the rest of your life, so you keep looking and suffer through some more searches, applications, and interviews. You may ultimately find a job in the industry that you have always wanted to be part of. That's a great accomplishment. But then, you start desiring to climb the corporate ladder: you want to move up from assistant to unit director, from unit director to department manager, and from department manager to area vice-president. Each step is a process of gaining something and losing something else, and to variable degrees, some of us will suffer more and others less in order to attain what we desire.

The Third Noble Truth, which affirms that suffering can be ended, is an important one. You have the ability to free yourself from much of your suffering, but you have to understand that it might require a step up in awareness. That means that you will have to engage in critical thinking. Seriously critical. You will have to take a critical look at your life and your desires and analyze whether you really want them to cause you suffering. In doing so, you may have to drill deep inside and question the reasons why you want what you want. Very often, your desires have been dictated by expectations outside yourself. It may be that your parents, peers, or even community expect you to evolve in a certain way and embark upon a particular career such as an attorney at law, a medical doctor, or an economist, and you simply never questioned if this is also what you would want.

When I was young, I wanted to become a flight attendant. My father was not too fond of that idea, because he wanted me to study and become an optometrist. Fortunately, neither the flight attendance nor the optometry career happened for me: I found out—in time—that flying was not my forte, and I realized that my math and physics skills were fine, but definitely not to the extent that I could utilize them as a foundation for my profession. In hindsight I realize that while these careers might have been lucrative and enriching in their own ways, they were not in line with my true passion.

It can also be that you desired something at one stage in your life and have now landed at a point where that desire no longer makes sense. However, because you already had it embedded in your system, you continue to strive toward making it happen. Deep thinking can help you see things in the right perspective and give you courage to cease chasing people, positions, or possessions that really no longer make sense to you. It is important to realize that you will change and that things that once seemed like the most attractive thing to you just don't do it for you anymore.

In my younger years I wanted to be a radio and television host, so I became one. I thrived on the popularity that this career brought me and loved to hear or see my programs being aired. Yet, after 20 years of doing something I was so passionate about at one time, I realized that I had reached a point of fatigue. I wanted to get out and explore new challenges, so I started studying again and embarked upon a career in education. Yet, it took a lot of deep thinking and even more courage to end a lucrative career that had become nothing more than work. The money and the popularity were still great, but the internal satisfaction had waned tremendously, and a new desire had emerged to engage in something that I considered more meaningful: I had matured.

It may even be that you still desire something but that you will find, through deep thinking, that the trouble to get this desire achieved is simply not worth your while. You may, for instance, find that a position you desired for quite some time would demand too much of your time and efforts, now that your priorities have changed. Similarly, you may come to the realization that the achievement of a desire has lost its luster to you because your perspectives are now different, and what you used to consider important a few years ago no longer matters to you today. In other words, the person you were when the desire was ignited in you no longer exists, and the person you are today has moved on from that old desire and is aspiring different purposes and directions in life.

I recall the time that I fantasized about becoming a well-known singer. I had a good voice, and I knew that, if I really had pushed for it, given my connections in the media at the time, I might have had a chance to become known as a singer. Somehow, however, I also realized that the introvert in me would not enjoy standing on stage night after night. And since I had discovered that flying was not my thing either, I realized that there would just be too much to sacrifice in making a career in singing on stage successful. Knowing now what I know about myself, I am happy that I never seriously pushed for a singing career.

Each of the examples above illustrated that awareness is critical in obtaining insight and ending unnecessary suffering. Sometimes it will also require courage. Many people continue to suffer in their circumstances because they are afraid of failure. I know quite some people who are absolutely unhappy with their job, but don't dare to give it up because they have bills to pay. Continuing in a draining job also zaps their energy and disables them from creating the time to look for another job. After work, they just want to stretch out on the couch and watch television or play games until they fall asleep.

The Fourth Noble Truth is the most comprehensive one and also the most challenging one. It is also known as the Noble Eightfold Path, and it is considered one of the most important teachings of the Buddha. The eightfold path consists of eight actions that should be implemented simultaneously. So, not an eight-step action plan, but a collective union of interrelated behaviors that help in thinking and acting right.

The eightfold path consists of right understanding (also referred to as right view), right thought, right speech, right action, right livelihood, right effort, right mindfulness, and right concentration. Thich Nhat Hanh,[1] one of the most revered Buddhist monks in the world, does a great job of explaining the eight elements on the Path. He perceives right view as a deep understanding of the Four Noble Truths; right thought as a means to improve right view; right speech is a manifestation of right thought; and right action as a consequence of right view, right thought, and right speech, as well as the path toward right livelihood. Thich further evaluates right effort to be the energy that helps us walk on the Noble Eightfold Path. He states, "Our practice should be intelligent, based on Right Understanding of the teaching. It is not because we practice hard that we can say we are practicing Right Diligence" (p. 99). Thich considers right mindfulness to be the heart of the Buddha's teachings. He clarifies, "When we are mindful, our thinking is Right Thinking, our speech is Right Speech, and so on. Right Mindfulness is the energy that brings us back to the present moment" (p. 64). Finally explaining step eight on the Eightfold Path, right concentration, Thich affirms, "The practice of Right Concentration is to cultivate a mind that is one-pointed" (p. 105).

Each of the following chapters will review one aspect of the Noble Eightfold Path and highlight its importance through examples of well-known leaders and everyday people who try their best to practice it.

---

[1] Thich Nhat Hanh (1998). *The Heart of the Buddha's Teaching: Transforming Suffering into Peace, Joy, and Liberation.* Broadway Books, New York, NY.

Buddhist Practices and the Workplace

An important reason why Buddhism may have grown so much in popularity over the past decades, when it comes to workplace studies in the USA, may be because it satisfies opposing perspectives on what "spirituality at work" entails. Spirituality at work, sometimes simply referred to as "spirit at work," has been on the rise as a trend since the early 1990s, but there are still differences in perspectives around this trend. The differences pertain to the relationship between spirituality and religion. Some authors feel that spirituality is not necessarily related to religion. Those authors[2] argue that spirituality is something that should not be confined to religion, as it can also be about a sense of purpose, meaning, and connectedness to one another. Others feel that religion is the foundation of all spiritual practices. Some of those[3] consider that spirituality includes terms such as energy, meaning, and knowing and that it relates to the various spiritualities of Tao, Buddhism, Hinduism, Zen, and Native American spirituality. For both of the above perspectives, the pro-religious and the anti-religious view, Buddhism provides an acceptable passage, as it is oftentimes referred to as more of a psychology or ethical system, while some may prefer to see it as a religion.

As mentioned before, we approach Buddhism more as a psychology or ethical system—a philosophy—in this book. When Buddhist practices are not approached as a religion, they become widely acceptable because they make very much sense in a secular perspective.

It is particularly the fact that Buddhism focuses on mindfulness or greater awareness, sometimes also referred to as consciousness, that makes it so appealing in today's workplaces. In his book *The New Buddhism*, David Brazier[4] confirms that Buddhism goes beyond subjective concerns, or even altered states of consciousness, in order to reach the real world. There are few philosophies, or religions, that have focused so deeply and extensively on consciousness as Buddhism. Brazier is of the opinion that the Buddha, through his teachings, was calling for a revolution in human consciousness. This emphasis on human consciousness is still abundantly present in modern days' Buddhist teachings, as we can conclude from the following example:

---

[2] Giacalone, R.A. & Jurkiewicz, C.L. (2003). Toward a science of workplace spirituality, in Giacalone, R.A. & Jurkiewicz, C.L. (Eds), *Handbook of Workplace Spirituality and Organizational Performance*, M.E. Sharpe, New York, NY.; Marques, J. (2005). Yearning for a more spiritual workplace. *Journal of American Academy of Business, 7*(1), 149–53.

[3] Korac-Kakabadse, N., Kouzmin, A. & Kakabadse, A. (2002). Spirituality and leadership Praxis. *Journal of Managerial Psychology, 17*(3), 165–82.

[4] Brazier, D. (2002). *The New Buddhism*. Palgrave, New York, NY.

Our consciousness can be transformed at its base through the practice of mindful consuming, mindfully guarding our senses, and looking deeply. The practice should aim at transforming both the individual and the collective aspects of our consciousness.[5]

Buddhism's focus on consciousness aims to peel off the layer of ignorance and mindless acceptance of the status quo, in which we have been conditioned through modern society, elevate us from the ignorance of going through our daily motions as if we were sleepwalking, and rise to expanded awareness. Thich stresses that, when our ignorance has been transformed, our consciousness becomes wisdom.

Many people wonder whether there should be any place for religion in work environments.

Well, perhaps it might not be appropriate as a group activity. Religion should not be shoved down anyone's throat, and people should definitely be left the freedom to choose which religion they want to adhere to without forcing it onto others. In workplaces, particularly, the dominant display of one religion especially by individuals in leadership positions can create inhibitions among workers who hold other beliefs or serve as a concealed message to them to openly start enforcing theirs as well. Consequently, this could lead to alienation and the familiar and highly despised in- and out-group situation, whereby members of the leader's religion would become part of the in-group, and all others would remain in the out-group.

This is exactly why we don't approach Buddhism as a religion in this book, but rather as a practical method that can be practiced by members of all religions as well as those who prefer not to adhere to any religion at all.

Within the philosophical approach of Buddhism, there is no worship of any God or upper being. And yet, while this book reviews Buddhist practices as a set of ethical guidelines, there is no escaping to the fact that it is still very much considered a religion by many. So, let us use this section of the chapter to consider five critical attention points of Buddhist when perceived as a religion, especially in the USA.

1. *The level of religiousness in the US society.* When we look at the perspectives toward religion in human interaction, we detect a contradiction, especially in a country driven as highly by religious convictions as North America.

---

[5] Thich Nhat Hanh (1998). *The Heart of the Buddha's Teaching: Transforming Suffering into Peace, Joy, and Liberation.* Broadway Books, New York, NY.

More than 90% of US citizens believe in God or a higher power,[6] which makes this nation one of the most religious ones in the world. Of course, religion entails much more than just believing in God, but in America, the predominant way of religious practices is linked to Christian-based denominations and, therefore, belief in God.

When we bring the workplace into scope, we see that there is resurgence of religion's place in the USA because, in recent decades, the traditional wall against this trend has been crumbling.[7] This can be attributed to a number of factors, such as the increasing role of work in our daily life and the growing belief among US workers that greed is the most important driver of US business leaders. And then there is also the fact that there is a blurred definition of what exactly religion is these days. Now, within this increased prominence of religion at work, Buddhism plays an interesting role. On one hand, Buddhist practices seem to appeal to many, and on the other hand, we have the fact that there is no force to change one's existing beliefs while also embracing Buddhist behaviors. Now that there are more women and minority members in the US workforce, the diversity of religions has increased, and so has the confusion.

Many business leaders oppose the spirituality movement, especially when religion comes into view, claiming that it distracts attention from the real purpose of business, which to them is still the bottom line. In more recent years, some shrewd business leaders have started to buy into the concept of workplace spirituality and some other leniencies toward religion at work based on the mindset that happy workers will perform better. In popular terms, "If you give them what they want, they will give you want you want."

2. *Increased tensions and conflict.* As discussed above, we are dealing with a combination of more diversity in religions in the USA, a greater level of acceptance of religious practices in the workplace, and mixed opinions about these trends, we get a growing degree of tension and conflicts. Employees who are confronted with religious practices at work that are not in line with their own may feel harassed, but may also realize that it is not so easy to object against a religious practice, because this may lead to being alienated or even losing their job!

Workplace supervisors might consider educating themselves on religious do's and don'ts of their employees. In addition, supervisors should

---

[6] Morgan, J.F. (2005). In defense of the workplace religious freedom act: protecting the unprotected without sanctifying the workplace. *Labor Law Journal, 56*(1), 68–71.

[7] Ibid.

remain aware of the rights of workers, toward religious expressions, stay abreast of court decisions on the religious issue, and include these decisions in handbooks and policy documents while also keeping meticulous notes on religious issues as they occur among workers.[8] Yet, regardless of how many precautions supervisors try to take, there is still plenty of room to fail, because organizational environments, workers, and cultures differ tremendously. It may be wisest for supervisors in today's US workplaces to remain accessible toward workers, limit expression of their own religious convictions in order to set an example, express their willingness to respect and accept religious practices within reasonable bounds, and nurture an open communication flow with employees.

3. *Western interpretations and implementations of Buddhism.* Several students of Buddhism have observed that western societies changed the purpose of Buddhism from a social religion to a solitary practice. With that, they took Buddhist practice away from the traditional Sangha environment and made it more leaning toward new-age mysticism.[9] These Buddhist observers feel that in highly industrialized countries such as Japan and the USA, Buddhism has become a handy training tool to suppress workers' dissatisfaction and distract attention from corporate malpractice. Some of these observers criticize Buddhism along the lines of Christianity, in that they believe it has taught its followers to accept suffering when they should not. The critics point out that when followers perceive their suffering as a price they pay for wrongdoings from previous lives (karma), they don't do anything to improve their circumstances. The critics also feel that Buddhist psychology is too idealistic in that it only caters to individuals with a higher level of intellectual development. People with higher intellectual levels use Buddhism to enhance their sense of social sensitivity, while the masses, with their limited levels of comprehension and resources, do not really benefit from this religion.

The concerns above are only partly justified. Buddhism is often defined within two vehicles: the larger vehicle (Mahayana), and the smaller but older vehicle (Theravada). Theravada has always been a practice of seclusion. Besides, it might not be too much of a concern that Buddhism is

---

[8] Montgomery, J.G. (2002). A most delicate matter: religious issues and conflict in the US library Workplace. *Library Management, 23*(8/9), 422–32.

[9] Crabtree, V. (2004). Criticism of Buddhism, Vexen Crabtree. Retrieved from: www.vexen.co.uk/religion/buddhism_criticism.html; Fields, R. (1998). Divided dharma: white Buddhists, ethnic Buddhists, and racism, in Prebish, C.S. & Tanaka, K.K. (Eds), *The Faces of Buddhism in America*, University of California Press, Berkely and Los Angeles, CA, pp. 196–206; Nattier, J. (1997). Buddhism comes to Main Street. *The Wilson Quarterly, 21*(2), 72–80; Numrich, P.D. (2003). Two Buddhisms further considered. *Contemporary Buddhism, 4*(1), 55–78.

taking on different shapes in different places. The Dalai Lama often praises the flexibility of Buddhism and attributes its ability to remain intact throughout multiple millennia to the fact that it can be adapted to the perceptions of local societies. As for the understanding that karma transcends multiple lifetimes, Buddhist scholars agree that there is a perception that we pay for our wrongdoings of previous lives, but at the same time, Buddhism also teaches that we can improve our karma by actually engaging in proper actions toward betterment.

4. *Killing Buddhism as a religion and establishing it as a contemplative science.* This suggestion is based on the fact that, over time, religions often move away from their initial purpose and lead to violence.[10] To proponents of this argument feel that Buddhism is a set of ethical principles and meditation, revealing valuable truths about the mind and the phenomenal world. Some of these truths are emptiness, selflessness, and impermanence. These truths are not limited to "Buddhist" thinking, so the notion of a "religion" toward Buddhism stands in the way of potential success that its philosophical underpinnings could have for humanity.

Other western authors agree that there is nothing to be concerned about in Buddhism and Confucianism and that these should not be treated as religions but as ethical systems or philosophies of life.[11] Indeed, when perceiving Buddhism as a set of ethical rules toward improved leadership of the self and better interactions with others, it makes infinitely more sense and has a much better chance of being accepted at a larger scale than when it is restrained by the boundaries of religious dogma, thereby alienating those that are already devoted to one particular religion or those who are averse to any kind of religion.

In his book, *The New Buddhism: The Western Transformation of an Ancient Tradition*, James Coleman[12] points out clearly the problem with religion. He starts out by explaining that Buddha himself was not a Buddhist, but just a man who woke up, saw things as they were, and wanted to help others see the truth also. He then stresses that it were "the institutional structures and traditions" that emerged around Siddhartha Gautama's (the Buddha) teachings that made Buddhism into what we traditionally call a religion. Coleman then refers to the German sociologist Max Weber's perspective that a religion gets "routinized" once the charismatic teacher dies.

[10] Harris, S. (2006). Killing the Buddha. *Shambala Sun*. Retrieved from www.shambhalasun.com/index. php?option¼com_content&task¼view&id¼2903&Itemid¼0

[11] Dawkins, R. (2006). *The God Delusion*. Houghton Mifflin, New York, NY.

[12] Coleman, J.W. (2002). *The New Buddhism: The Western Transformation of an Ancient Tradition*. Oxford University Press, New York, NY.

It is this "routinization" that is considered a burden to not only Buddhism but to all religions. David Hawkins made a similar point at least three of his books: *Power vs Force, The Eye of the I,* and *I: Reality and Subjectivity.*[13] Hawkins pointed out that religions, and all other ideologies for that matter, start with good intentions from a charismatic and highly intelligent individual. Unfortunately, they get dispersed by less insightful individuals who do not have a full grasp of the essence of the initial ideology. With their limited insights, these individuals then structure and "routinize" the theory, thus establishing rules and regulations that were never intended by the original teacher. The biggest problem to all of this is that the structures become an end onto themselves, so that ultimately the letter is preserved and not the spirit of the teaching.

5. *Americanization of Buddhism.* It seems that the question whether Buddhism has a proper place in the capitalistic American world of work has been contemplated by several prominent Buddhists. In *Dharma and Greed: Popular Buddhism Meets the American Dream,* David Templeton[14] presents the question as to whether someone can be truly Buddhist while being truly American. He does so after observing the obvious contradictions between the Buddhist ideals of social behavior, moderation, and transcending greed and envy and the American way of living, which is exactly based on the opposite: individualism, affluence, greed, and envy. Templeton reviews a meeting held in June 2000, in which 220 prominent Buddhist leaders in America participated and in which the Dalai Lama partook as well. Templeton reports that the Dalai Lama was informed about the fact that, in the USA, Buddhism mainly appealed to more intellectual and affluent Americans who could afford expensive retreats and pricey Buddhist paraphernalia: the "spiritual" materialists.

As a consequence, the Dalai Lama stressed that Buddhist practitioners in the USA should still focus on compassion and freedom of anger and greed, even in a money-mad nation as America. Subsequently reviewing an American Buddhist business person, Peter Bermudes, who is the director of a Boston-based Buddhist book publishing company—a nonprofit entity that makes a healthy living because Buddhist literature sells great in

---

[13] Hawkins, D.R. (1995). *Power vs Force: The Hidden Determinants of Human Behavior.* Hayhouse Inc, Carlsbad, CA.; Hawkins, D.R. (2001). *The Eye of the I: From Which Nothing is Hidden.* Veritas Publishing, West Sedona, AZ.; Hawkins, D.R. (2003). *I: Reality and Subjectivity.* Veritas Publishing, West Sedona, AZ.

[14] Templeton, D. (2000). *Dharma & Greed: Popular Buddhism Meets the American Dream.* Metro Publishing Inc, Northern California Bohemian, CA. Retrieved from www.metroactive.com/papers/sonoma/10.12.00/buddhism-0041.html

America—Templeton (2000) draws the conclusion that most American Buddhists are independent practitioners. They read books and do not feel compelled to be part of a congregation of any sort. Templeton further analyzes other American Buddhist ventures, such as Greyston Bakery in New York, and finds that the combination of being commercial while still adhering to spiritual values is possible, even though it requires thorough and regular self-examination. Templeton leaves the question whether being truly Buddhist while being truly American is possible unanswered. Templeton's comments are also included in Allan Holender's book *Zentrepreneurism*, in which Holender introduces a number of new terms such as zentrepreneurism, zenployees, and zenvesting in an attempt to combine Buddhist virtues to American commercialism.[15]

The earlier raised and unanswered query by Templeton about a potential incompatibility between being Buddhist and being American is a specifically interesting one when we consider it in light of the two earlier mentioned main streams of Buddhism, Theravada and Mahayana. Theravada Buddhism, the school of the elders, teaches that only a precious few will ever attain enlightenment. Within this view, there has only been one Buddha, which entails that there should be no expectations of enlightened behavior among mainstream Buddhist practitioners. The self-focused, independent mentality of American Buddhist practitioners, who are predominantly affluent intellectuals, might therefore not be considered as particularly disturbing within the Theravada concept. However, it is within the Mahayana concept, which also known as "great vehicle," that perceptual discrepancies may arise. Mahayana teaches that enlightenment can be obtained by everyone and that there are enlightened beings or Bodhisattvas all around us, who strongly focus on being compassionate toward others, thus decreasing selfish behavior and increasing their awareness of interconnectedness with all living beings. As the Dalai Lama is considered a Mahayana Buddhist (Tibetans are often referred to as Vajrayana or Tantrayana Buddhists, which are derivatives of the Mahayana stream), this development should be considered a rather interesting one.

In his review presented above, Templeton stressed that the Dalai Lama has been informed about the self-centered practices of contemporary American Buddhists and that he has urged for more compassion and less greed. However, time will be the only discloser about the ultimate direction of American Buddhism. A compelling tentative conclusion to be drawn

---

[15] Holender, A. (2008). *Zentrepreneurism: A Twenty-First Century Guide to the New World of Business*. Book Tree, New York, NY.

from this development is that while most of the affluent, intellectual Americans were initially attracted to Buddhism through Tibetan (Mahayana-based) teachers, they ultimately seem to fit more within the Theravada concept, which does not require actions such as generosity and compassion as prevalent elements of daily practices. The multiple visits of the Dalai Lama to the USA, along with his numerous books and presentations, could very well be seen as a concerted effort to instill a behavioral transformation among American Buddhist toward increased compassion and generosity. At the same time, it should be emphasized that the Dalai Lama has often declared that Buddhism has survived over the course of so many centuries due to its flexibility to adapt to local cultures. Within that perspective, it may be assumed that the Dalai Lama, while continuously encouraging the Bodhisattva ideal, will refrain from deliberately manipulating the development of American Buddhism in one way or another.

Aside from the five contemplations presented above, it could be concluded that the increased popularity of Buddhism in America may be attributed to the fact that it fits in well with the contemporary trend of greater awareness, environmental sustainability, and increased social responsibility. Buddhism forms a welcome response to the call for spirituality at work, which is fueled by a number of factors such as increased diversity in US workplaces, greater insight into and aversion toward the greed of many American corporate leaders, and a desire toward greater satisfaction at work. Bookstores, online sources, and management speakers capitalize cunningly onto this trend and gear their product offerings heavily on this need.

In the middle of this all emerges Buddhism, now even more than before, as the Dalai Lama, the most prominent Buddhist personality, travels and speaks throughout the world, publishes one book after the other, and gains popularity among American celebrities. It is difficult, at this point in time, to distinguish whether the current flare of Buddhism in America will merely be a fad that will subside as soon as a new one emerges or whether this trend should be seen within the greater scope of increased human, thus also American, awareness against the developments of the twenty-first century: greater access to information, more international human interaction, and enhancement in conscious choice making. The series of occurrences to which the US society has been exposed in the past century and since the start of this millennium may also have ignited a serious urge among Americans to rethink the conventional US way of careless spending, adhering to external appearances, and mindlessly following trends. All these occurrences may have contributed toward the creation of a fertile foundation for a change of mentality in the USA, to which Buddhism may be a useful inspiration. So, while the Americanization of Buddhism is a fact, it may also be that Americans are deviating from their traditional ways (de-Americanizing) and redefining themselves (re-Americanizing). This entails that the ultimate look and practice of "Americanized Buddhism" or "Buddhism Americana" is still in process of development.

3

Right View

It Couldn't Last

In the comfort of my quiet bliss
I close my eyes and reminisce
About life and its unpredictability:
A fusion of turmoil and tranquility.

The beauty of a brand new day
That can easily shift into disarray,
The many things I take for granted
The desires that keep me enchanted.

The aversions, which I seek to reject
The well of happiness I try to detect.
Mother Nature in her crudest form:
Today serene, tomorrow storm.

Life and death, illness and health;
Youth, old age, poverty and wealth.
All around, so much to cherish,
Too much, really, before I perish…

So, I close my eyes in gratitude,
And quietly celebrate this interlude
As this moment sinks into the past
I let it go. It couldn't last
                                        ~Joan Marques

© Springer Nature Switzerland AG 2019
J. Marques, *Lead with Heart in Mind*, https://doi.org/10.1007/978-3-030-17028-8_3

If you want to live right, you cannot implement just one or a few parts of the Noble Eightfold Path and ignore some other parts. In other words, you cannot work on having a right view, but then ignore what would be the right intention. You cannot practice right speech and then promptly engage in mindlessness. Yes, it happens a lot, and it's a challenge in today's hectic, demanding, fast-paced world to practice all elements of the Noble Eightfold Path, but it's the only way that you will be able to cross-check for yourself if you are on the right path: when all eight elements are in place, you know you are doing the right thing.

Right view is an essential part of the eightfold path, and—as will repeatedly be clarified—it should not be seen as part of a sequence of actions, but rather a segment of an interconnected whole.[1] Right view has been described as "seeing a thing in its true nature, without name and label".[2]

Holding the right view of anything means to do away with negativity, mean-spiritedness, spitefulness, and prejudice. Now, this is harder than you would think, because we all carry certain prejudices in us, whether those were instilled by our upbringing, our culture, our friends, our beliefs, or any other resource. Indeed, it is not so simple to hold a right view, and because of that, grant an opportunity for a job to a stranger with better qualifications than your friend's son. But don't judge too fast: sometimes there may be good reasons to give your friend's son a chance over someone with better qualifications: the youngster may have gone through tremendous hardship and could genuinely use a hand up, for instance. This example shows that "right view" is a personal thing. What you will consider the right view depends on the mental, emotional, and spiritual place where you currently stand. Yet, as long as you can live with this view and as long as you have thought about it deeply and are convinced that it will lead to the right action, you should be fine.

There is an old story about the right view and how you obtain and behold it. It's about an old man who taught a younger one that there are two wolves in each of us. The wolves continuously fight each other. One wolf signifies your jealousy, meanness, spite, anger, negativity, and hate. The other wolf is your generosity, tolerance, understanding, peace, and harmony. The wolf that wins is the one that you feed. That wolf will also determine your view. Will your view be driven by the first set of emotions or by the second set? If you think about it, this means that your view determines your attitude. It influences the choices you make, the way you see things, and the way you act upon them.

---

[1] O'Brien, B. (Sept. 1, 2017). Right View—The Buddhist Eightfold Path. ThoughtCo. Retrieved from https://www.thoughtco.com/right-view-450073
[2] Rahula, W. (1974). *What the Buddha Taught*. Grove Press, NY., p. 49.

Elon Musk and the Greater Purpose of Doing Business

How Blessings Are Earned

Give the gift of love, because the world needs it
Give the gift of peace: you'll find it in your heart
Give the gift of support, because someone deserves it
Give the gift of knowledge, because you're smart

Give the gift of listening: you can, because you care
Give the gift of affection, as it warms all around
Give the gift of good thoughts, even if no one sees them
Give the gift of sharing: it's a hard one to be found

Give the gift of truth: it's almost wiped out today
Give the gift of trust, and you'll find it is returned
Give the gift of goodwill, as a dedicated human
Give the gift of giving: it's how blessings are earned
                                        –Joan Marques

If you consider yourself a leader, your right view will have to guarantee well-being for a large group of stakeholders, and not just your own pockets or those whom you surround yourself with. Elon Musk is a well-known leader of our times who did just that: he consciously and systematically devoted all his business projects to meeting the needs of society. Musk's "right view" began with Tesla electric cars, a project that had been attempted several times before, but never to the magnitude of Musk's efforts. His view was to decrease and someday cease the unsustainable use of fossil fuels. Next, Musk joined the renewable energy movement and co-founded SolarCity, because he had a vision to improve environmental responsibility and reduce costs for electricity. Meanwhile, he also got involved in SpaceX, because he wanted to do something about a problem that everyone had only been talking about with growing concern: the overpopulation of the Earth. Through SpaceX, Musk wanted to prepare us for a potential investigation of Mars as an alternative home for humanity.

The way Elon Musk implements "right view" is by looking at, and thinking about, the major challenges our human society faces. If you consider this further, you can also see the connection with the other elements of the Noble Eightfold Path: through his right view, which he obtained through right mindfulness and right concentration, he develops the right intention, finds the inspiration to convince others for his projects through right speech, creates momentum to engage in right effort which becomes right action, and then starts working on his projects, thus generating right livelihood.

Elon Musk's right view happens on a global scale: he embarks upon major projects with the aim to solve major problems that others may not readily consider, or may not dare to tackle, because they are so immense. Several authors, who have written about Musk, claim that this man holds truly revolutionary views about our collective future, with visions that are decades ahead of their time.[3] Musk had acquired the reputation of being a visionary long before his mass society-improvement projects Tesla, SolarCity, and SpaceX. He was one of the success stories of the dot.com era with ventures such as Zip2 and X.com. He managed to sell Zip2 to Compaq Computers for more than $300 million and sold X.com, the forerunner of PayPal, to E-Bay for $1.5 billion. These early windfalls paved the way for him to think bigger and broader and consider real major problems in the world to address.

Let's be honest: how many people look at the problems that our civilization has created and actually try to correct them? Especially issues of an environmental nature that often give us a feeling of powerlessness, because they require such an immense change and will trigger so much opposition from the richest and most powerful in society, because they own most of the major factories that are responsible for pollution and contamination? Is there, then, really a major complaint to be uttered if someone steps up and steers us toward cleaner air and reduced depletion of scarce resources?

One way in which Musk also practices right view is that he doesn't cling to his patents. Initially, he was afraid that Tesla would be crushed by the major automakers, who would copy the technology and flood the market with their products, so that he would be pushed out of business. By 2014, Musk realized that such was not the case. On the contrary, up till that time, the major automakers did not even use 1% of their capacity to produce zero emission cars. So, Musk realized that if he wanted to help keep our air cleaner, he should do the right thing, and he did that by releasing his patents. He did so, because he realized that if Tesla and other car makers would start making more electric cars, the world would benefit from a common, rapidly evolving technology platform.

Just like Steve Jobs, the legendary brain behind Apple computers, Musk is more a visionary than an inventor: he takes existing knowledge and applies it

[3] Vance, A. (2012). Elon Musk, Man of Tomorrow. (cover story). *Business Week*, (4296), 73–79.

in ways not successfully implemented before. He has the ability to look at a problem or a new development and see solutions and applications that others have not yet considered. Some people have even called him the greatest optimist in history, because he seems to believe that any problem that does not infringe with the law of physics can be solved.[4] And while he makes good money doing what he's doing, it is admirable that Elon Musk continues to try to bring well-being to all living beings on our common planet. That is a great example of practicing right view.

Ayah Bdeir and LittleBits

Obsolete Program

We're programmed to compete
Against our sisters and brothers
We're programmed to get ahead
At the dreadful expense of others
We're programmed to wish
Bad luck upon our rival
We're programmed to think
That superiority equals revival

We're programmed to develop
Ego's of gigantic sizes
We're programmed to look down
On everyone who's in crisis
We're programmed to chase wealth
And achieve it at any cost
We're programmed to build walls
That help us to get others lost

We're programmed to march along
In a parade we may not even like
We're programmed to accept
That our life's a hopeless hike
We're programmed to tolerate
Hierarchies, in-groups, and strife
We're programmed to favor
A dollar over the rescue of a life

---

[4] Vandermey, A. (2013). The shared genius of Elon Musk and Steve Jobs. *Fortune, 168* (9), 98.

We're programmed to ignore
That we're firmly conditioned
We're programmed to believe
That we're immovably positioned
We're programmed to think
That this is all there is
We're programmed not to question
Whether anything's amiss

But if we really want
We can escape this mental penitentiary
That was a dark-aged invention
And doesn't work in the 21st century
It's time for increased awareness
To turn the tide of annihilation
And lead us back on the path
Of mutual respect and salvation
                                    ~Joan Marques

Of course there are also people of lesser fame than Elon Musk who practice right view. A person that seems to have the ability to practice right view and whose actions we should follow is Ayah Bdeir, a Lebanese Canadian, who founded LittleBits, an open-source system of small, preassembled, modular circuits that snap together with magnets.

Ayah was born in Montreal, Canada, in 1982 and raised in Beirut, Lebanon. Her late father was an entrepreneur and her mother a banker. Ayah has repeatedly expressed gratitude to her parents for raising her and her sisters in a world where science was promoted. This is how the girls fell in love with mathematics, science, and design and were able to pursue their passions in the professional areas of their choice. The signs were rather clear as Ayah was growing up: as a girl she would take things apart in order to see what was inside. Her parents were not hung up on gender differences and inspired the girls to become scientists and engineers and become career women. Ayah received firsthand motivation to attend college from her mother, who pursued her own degree while her daughters were in school. Today, she can proudly refer to herself as an engineer and interactive artist and, more precisely, as the founder and CEO of LittleBits. Ayah has earned countless awards for her work, including acquisition into the MoMA (Museum of Modern Art) permanent collection.

LittleBits' mission is to put the power of electronics in the hands of everyone and to break down complex technologies so that anyone can build, prototype, and invent. Because of the magnets, it's easy to know which sides snap together and which reject one another, so even children can become very creative with LittleBits, even if they don't have any engineering experience. By developing and making LittleBits accessible to everyone (it's open source, remember), Ayah has created a way to make learning about electronics fun, easy, and creative.[5] Part of the millennial generation, Bdeir is already considered one of the leaders of movements in which creative resources are made widely available at no cost, such as the Maker Movement and the Open Hardware Movement. She claims that her mission is to democratize hardware, and, indeed, Ayah Bdeir has been widely praised for her great ideas and even more for the visionary, generous approach of sharing the outcomes of her creative insights to anyone who might be interested.

Similar to Elon Musk, Ayah Bdeir's approach appeals to many, most likely because of the greater purpose behind its existence: LittleBits aims to bring progress to as wide a group of people possible - all over the world - and is secure enough in its mission to share the "recipe" of its product with anyone interested. On top of that, LittleBits crosses boundaries by bringing engineering and art together. For those reasons, LittleBits has experienced rapid growth, raising $44.2 million in Series B funding in 2015, thus bringing its total capital raised to nearly $60 million within 2 years after creation. The company sells its electronic building blocks for students and hobbyists in 130 countries and works with more than 3500 schools.[6] LittleBits produces about 50 different modules that can be purchased individually or in kits. There are four types of modules in different lengths and with different functions: the blue ones provide power; the pink ones are for inputs, such as switches, microphones, and motion sensors; the green ones are for outputs such as lights, motors, and speakers; and the orange ones provide wires or logic functions. The modules are designed in such a way that they fit together magnetically, so that the circuits can be joined correctly.[7]

---

[5] Tupper, T. (Oct 9, 2015). Ayah Bdeir founded littleBits to make science fun. She might now be on to something bigger. *Forbes Business*. Retrieved from https://www.forbes.com/sites/forbesinternational/2015/10/09/ayah-bdeir-founded-littlebits-to-make-science-fun-she-might-now-be-on-to-something-bigger/#3c53da178b3d

[6] Henry, Z. (January 12, 2018). This Startup Founder Offers Up the Perfect Response to Trump's Travel Ban Ayah Bdeir, the founder and CEO of LittleBits, wants to counter the perception of Arabic as 'the other.' *Inc.* Retrieved from https://www.inc.com/zoe-henry/how-littlebits-founder-ayah-bdeir-pushing-back-against-trump-immigration-ban.html

[7] Schaffer, A. (2014). Ayah Bdeir, 31: Electronic blocks that link with one another also connect art and engineering. *TechnologyReview*. Retrieved from https://www.technologyreview.com/lists/innovators-under-35/2014/entrepreneur/ayah-bdeir/

Martin Luther King and His Dream

The Soul of Love

The soul of love is in the self
It's captured in the heart
It can't be stored on ledge or shelf
It can't be torn apart

The soul of love is wholesome too
It adds esteem to life
It flourishes when hearts are true
It helps boon to survive

The soul of love has angel wings
To fly away from pain
It touches long forgotten strings
It never works in vain

The soul of love transcends through time
It never gets too old
It's everlasting in its prime
And never does grow cold

The soul of love should never die
No matter if we do
It should still be when seas run dry
And sky's no longer blue

The soul of love is like a breath
It's quiet, but it's there
Let's keep it from just going death
And spread it everywhere
~Joan Marques

I have the audacity to believe that peoples everywhere can have three meals a day for their bodies, education and culture of their minds, and dignity, equality, and freedom for their spirits. I believe that what self-centered men have torn down, men other-centered can build up. I still believe that one day mankind will bow before the altars of God and be crowned triumphant over war and bloodshed, and nonviolent redemptive goodwill will proclaim the rule of the land (MLK, from his Nobel Peace Prize Acceptance Speech).[8]

To show you that "right view" is definitely not only limited to business but that it has a positive impact when and where applied, let's consider Dr. Martin Luther King, an American Baptist minister and activist who became the most prominent representative and leader in the nation's civil rights movement till date. King was also a visionary, who dealt with the civil rights movement in America like Mahatma Gandhi had done in India: through non-violence. He devoted most of his adult years to the struggle against racial inequality in the USA, leading bus boycotts, anti-segregation walks, fair housing demonstrations, and of course The Great March on Washington in 1963, where he delivered his famous "I Have a Dream" speech to more than 200,000 civil rights marchers at the Lincoln Memorial in Washington, DC.

Dr. King's actions were closely intertwined with his view, as should always be the case. He was arrested numerous times for his efforts and sent to jail 29 times. Most of his arrests were either for acts of civil disobedience or for made-up charges, such as in Montgomery, Alabama, for driving 30 miles per hour in a 25-mile-per-hour zone. Yet, throughout it all, MLK did not allow the fear of being chastised and locked away inhibit his goal. There was a greater cause and there was much at stake. Large groups of people were hopeful of his views and dependent on the outcome of his actions, so he knew he could not give up. Throughout his struggle, it became apparent to King that he might have to pay a high price one day for his bravery, but there was no going back, and up till his assassination in 1968, he traveled through Southern and Northern states to help voice the need for change and equality, much to the displeasure of the supremacists, who expressed their hatred through different degrees of violence.[9]

The journey was not easy, and Dr. King has been accused of many things, some true and others untrue, but he was a hero in his own right, becoming the youngest recipient at the time to receive the Nobel Peace Prize, for combating racial inequality through nonviolent resistance. The year was 1964. During as well as after his life, MLK received many accolades for his right view, which changed the course of history in the USA. He was assassinated in Memphis, Tennessee, in 1968, at the age of 39.

---

[8] King, M. L. (December 10, 1964). Martin Luther King Jr. - Acceptance Speech. *Nobel Peace Prize Acceptance Speech.* Retrieved from https://www.nobelprize.org/nobel_prizes/peace/laureates/1964/king-acceptance_en.html

[9] Waxman, O. (January 12, 2018). The Surprising Story Behind This Shocking Photo of Martin Luther King Jr. Under Attack. *Time.* Retrieved from http://time.com/5096937/martin-luther-king-jr-picture-chicago/

The Right View Movement Is On

There is a wonderful upsurge of people from all walks of life that join the right view movement with sustainable solutions for practices that have thus far been unsustainable. Consider innovator-entrepreneur Scott Munguia, who designed a technology for the production of bioplastics from avocado seeds. Bioplastics are plastics made from renewable biomass sources, such as vegetable fats and oils, which biodegrade more readily than the so far used fossil fuel-based plastics. By using avocado seeds, Scott offers a world-changing solution in multiple dimensions: not only does he produce a biodegradable product, but he also addresses a major problem in Mexico, where his company is located; he helps reduce about 30,000 ton of avocado seeds, which were thus far considered agro-industrial waste.

How it started? Scott read a paper that depicted a picture of the corn molecule, frequently used to make bioplastic. Since he was familiar with the avocado seed molecule, his mind made the link, and a great idea was conceived! It took 2 years of preparation, but the prospects are good: Mexico produces about half of the world's supply of avocados, and the world market for bioplastic is immense: $5.8 billion.[10]

Scott, who is still a student of chemical engineering at the time of this writing, plans to build his company, Biofase, in Michoacán, a highly affected region. He has already won several awards internationally and locally for his innovative and broadly useful views.[11]

And how about Eyad Janneh, who was raised in Syria, but now works with *Field Ready*, a nonprofit humanitarian organization operating from Istanbul, Turkey. Field Ready prepares locally made humanitarian supplies to help alleviate existing needs. Eyad's team designs and tests tools that can be made on location from available materials. In 2017 one of these airbags was used in Syria to help rescue two people trapped in rubble. Eyad was listed on the 2017 list of 35 innovators under 35 as a humanitarian innovator to watch.[12]

It's impossible to tell how the future will unfold for the young dynamic minds discussed in this chapter, Ayah, Scott, and Eyad, or even for Elon Musk

---

[10] MacBride, E. (April 30, 2015). Avocado Seeds Into Plastic: A Mexican Chemical Engineer Aims At $5.8B Market. *Forbes*. Retrieved from https://www.forbes.com/sites/elizabethmacbride/2015/04/30/avocado-seeds-into-plastic-a-mexican-chemical-engineer-aims-at-5-8b-market/#6c65659b5482

[11] *Innovators Under 35* (2018). Scott Munguía. MIT Technology Review. Retrieved from http://old.innovatorsunder35.com/innovator/scott-mungu%C3%ADa

[12] 35 Innovators under 35. Humanitarians: Finding the technology solutions that can directly improve, and sometimes save, people's lives - Eyad Janneh. *MIT Technology Review 2017*. Retrieved from https://www.technologyreview.com/lists/innovators-under-35/2017/humanitarian/suchi-saria/

for that matter. The future is a big unknown, and these people can become globally known entities or get lost in obscurity, but at the moment of writing this work, they stood as great examples for the right view that we can all develop if we want to do so. And as has been demonstrated by Elon Musk and Ayah Bdeir, there is always enthusiastic buy-in for great ideas that can elevate the quality of life on Earth. Developing and maintaining the right view, as these examples also demonstrated, invariably leads to right intention, right speech, right action, right livelihood, right effort, right mindfulness, and right concentration.

None of the people described in this chapter, nor the ones we will review in the following chapters, are or were saints, but they made or hope to make an important contribution to the wellness in their society, and that is what right view is all about.

4

Right Intention

Why Not?

One moment
One precious moment

Where every living being,
Human and non-human,
Lives without torture, pain, or death
A moment in which we all rejoice
In the luxury of a griefless breath

Where our collective contentment
Peaks at its max: without reduction
No predators or preys, wins or losses
Wholesome and perfect: no destruction

Touching the heart of all life there is
In a moment of meditation and prayer
Aligning our minds in solemn serenity
Not just here or there, but everywhere

Could such a marvelous moment be?
Well, if everything starts with a thought,
Why not?

~Joan Marques

© Springer Nature Switzerland AG 2019
J. Marques, *Lead with Heart in Mind*, https://doi.org/10.1007/978-3-030-17028-8_4

Right intention is sometimes also referred to as "right thinking" or "right thought," and the context is the same: you have to focus consciously and refrain from making decisions that are based on questionable motives. Because right view and right intention depend so much on your mental state, they are often classified as the wisdom aspects in the eightfold path. Right intention is wonderful, but it can be rather challenging, because there will always be factors that steer you in different ways, causing you to overlook or forget your real motives.

Thich Nhat Hanh, a very prominent Buddhist monk, has developed four simple activities[1] that are very helpful in case you wonder if you still maintain right intention:

1. Always question what you see, hear, or read. Things can seem one way, but if you think deeper on them, you may realize that there are completely different interpretations possible and that your first thought may have been hasty and incorrect. If you regularly take time to reflect on things, you may find that you will refocus and that your intentions become more in-tune with your conscience.
2. Take a pause regularly to ask yourself what you're doing and why. This seems like a silly exercise, but it will force you to take some distance from your actions and face the reasons behind them. In other words, rather than just doing things as if you're on autopilot, you examine your intentions behind your actions. This is a powerful way to practice critical thinking, and it can help you release behaviors and practices that you were just implementing mindlessly based on old habits, but that no longer make sense today.
3. Spend some time on a regular basis to consider your habits. Your habits can be a strong but unnoticed force toward the decisions you make and the actions you take. Just like all of us, you have good habits and some that you are less proud of. It is easy to give in to your habits without even questioning them. Especially the bad habits seem to stick their head up when you least need them, and they can taint critical courses of action. So, be alert of your behaviors and responses, and, just as in point two, try to find out what drives them.
4. Keep an awakened mind that always considers the well-being of others. Buddhists call this "Bodhicitta." Bodhicitta pertains to the intention to do well onto others and help them become happier, more fulfilled beings.

---

[1] Why 'Right Intention' Is Important in Buddhism: Wisdom and the Eightfold. Thought Co. Retrieved from https://www.thoughtco.com/right-intention-450069

A straightforward way of understanding right intention is through the three-way consideration, as explained by the Buddha: the intention of releasing unwholesome thoughts, the intention of good will, and the intention of harmlessness.[2]

Muhammad Yunus and Grameen Bank

Emotions

Fear: A sense of anguish you want to minimize
Shame: a humiliation you shouldn't emphasize
Anger: an inner fury that leaves you in a mess
Hate: a disgusting taste that brings a lot of stress
Guilt: always a remorseful consequence
Pride: a conceited whiff that makes you very tense

Misery from fear, shame, anger, hate, guilt and pride
Makes you want to mope, weep, grieve and hide

Love: a natural sense of embracing others
Peace: accepting them as sisters and brothers
Acceptance: constructing bridges of unity
Generosity: giving back to the community
Reflection: coming to terms with life's capricious ways
Forgiveness: releasing hurt and restoring happy days

Happiness results from taking these virtues as a guide
It is your gracious personal gift, and it resides inside
                                                    ~Joan Marques

Dr. Muhammad Yunus is not an average businessman. He is, up till now, the only businessman who ever became the recipient of the Nobel Peace Prize. It happened in 2006, and he shared the prize with none other than his brain-child, Grameen Bank, which he founded with the intention to alleviate the tragic poverty in his home country Bangladesh. Dr. Yunus, now formally retired, received a doctorate in Economics in the USA and first lectured in Tennessee. When Bangladesh became independent, he decided to return to his home country and help build up its economy.

---

[2] Bodhi, B. (1994). Chapter III: RIGHT INTENTION (Samma Sankappa). Retrieved from http://www.vipassana.com/resources/8fp3.php

In Bangladesh, he first briefly worked for the government, but considered his job rather boring, so he resigned and returned to academia, accepting a position of head of the economics department at Chittagong University. A heartbreaking famine swept through the nation, and the evidence was widely visible. As an involved citizen, Dr. Yunus had been active in several anti-poverty movements and had a keen eye for the needs of the people. By the mid-1970s, he had adopted the habit to make regular walks through the city of Jobra, near Chittagong University. Observing the activities around him, Yunus was touched and disturbed by the poverty he witnessed. As he started having conversations with some of these hardworking people, he became aware that, regardless of all their diligent efforts and hard work, many of them had little or no chance to make any progress, because they were dependent on private moneylenders. These individual loan sharks made sure that, after delivery of end products and return of the money borrowed, there was never enough left for the micro-entrepreneurs to make any kind of progress.

Reflecting on what he learned from the situation, Dr. Yunus decided to organize a research project with his economics students, in order to find out how much money the poor people in the nearby village owed to the money-lenders. The total amount was about $27.00. Intrigued about the fact that such hardworking people could not get a loan for such a small total amount from a bona fide financial institution, Dr. Yunus visited the local bank to investigate. That's when he learned what is now common knowledge: that poor people cannot get loans from the bank, because of the general perception that they—the poor people—are not creditworthy and because they have no collateral. This, then, reveals how an unhealthy cycle is perpetuated: poor people lack collateral to get money from the bank, so they loan from loan sharks, who charge exorbitant interest rates and ensure that these poor people cannot save in order to ever grow financially.

Disheartened about the unproductive vicious cycle kept intact by conventional financial institutions, Yunus decided to lend the poor entrepreneurs in the village some money out of his own pocket. In the weeks after starting this personal lending project, Dr. Yunus learned that, contrary to what the banks assumed, the small business people repaid him 100% of the money he lent them. Encouraged by the results of his research project, Yunus returned to the bank with his data, only to find that nothing would change the notion the bank had adopted. The idea was based on an old, established discernment, and there was no openness to change.

Over the next few years, Yunus realized that he would have to be the change he wanted to see in the world. He founded Grameen Bank (Village Bank), and the fight against poverty became real. Shortly after opening, the bank changed its strategy from mainly providing loans to men to maintaining a heavy focus on women. This was based on the realization that most women were using the loans toward a family business and economic advancement for their children. Today, Grameen Bank is operating in more than 100 countries and has granted loans to about $7 billion to more than 7 million borrowers, 97% of which are women.

After retiring as president of Grameen Bank, Dr. Yunus intensified his global travels to raise awareness on the fight against poverty, thus continuing to expand his intention of eradicating poverty someday on this Earth.

Brittany Wenger's Artificial Brain Technology

Hope

If hope is mere
Disappointment postponed
Then we are here
Like empty carcasses cloned
Then efforts are
A waste of time
So welcome war;
hello there, crime!

If hope is but
An empty farce
Then we should cut
Our aim at stars
And – from now on
Grow wild and cruel
Perceive the sun
As one big fool

But if – as some say
"Hope is life"
Then every day
Is worth a dive
In this great pool
Of sparkling chances
Personality being the tool
To stretch all fences.
                    ~Joan Marques

A young woman who has demonstrated the right intention toward humanity's well-being is Brittany Wenger, a college student who built an artificial brain to detect breast cancer in 2012 at the tender age of 17 years!

Born in 1994 in Columbus, Ohio, Brittany is part of a generation of constructive dreamers, determined to make the world a better place, and not allowing age, gender, or anything else to get in the way of that. She has already established herself as a great inspiration for upcoming youngsters to also do something great. Her invention could greatly assist in the treatment of serious diseases such as breast cancer and leukemia. Thanks to today's technology, Brittany has introduced a system of medical examinations that will help detect diseases earlier and be more affordable and efficient to both surgeons and patients.[3]

As is the case with most of us, Brittany witnessed in her family the suffering that diseases such as breast cancer and leukemia can bring. She wanted to find out if it could be possible to detect these terrible diseases earlier, in order to enhance the chances of those who were diagnosed with them. Brittany's program, generally known as "Cloud4Cancer," is one of the most promising methods of doing a biopsy to date. What she did is basically teach the computer to diagnose breast cancer.[4]

Brittany has a set of hardworking and encouraging parents to thank for becoming such a focused and committed woman. Her parents taught her not to settle for mediocrity. They kept telling her that she would do great things one day, and this reinforcement propelled her into the passionate and determined person she is today. She did her best in school and had a particular interest in science and technology. Once she learned about artificial intelligence, there was no stopping her. She started researching online and in textbooks and began to teach her computer to do things. The first action was an AI program that could play soccer. Yet, when her cousin became victimized by breast cancer, Brittany got an idea: if she could teach her computer playing soccer, she could also teach it to help in medical diagnostic processes. It took Brittany many months, but in 2012, she released the "Global Neural Network Cloud Service for Breast Cancer"—more popularly known as "Cloud4Cancer".[5]

Brittany submitted her invention to the Google Science Fair that year and won first prize. This "artificial brain" technology assesses tissue samples for breast cancer. Brittany's invention, Cloud4Cancer, determines with 99.11% accuracy whether a sample of breast tissue is malignant or benign using neural

---

[3] Horsfield, P. (2018). Brittany Wenger. *TheExtraordinary.org.* Retrieved from https://www.thextraordinary.org/brittany-wenger#biography
[4] Ibid.
[5] Ibid.

networks, code that imitates the way the human brain makes decisions.[6] Her intention is to help wipe out cancer completely. Yet, the learning process to the point where she could call her efforts an "invention" was a lengthy one, filled with trial and error. Brittany's interest in computer science started with an elective class on futuristic thinking. She became interested in technology of the future and started researching artificial intelligence and how it transcended into human knowledge. Next, she bought a coding textbook and slowly taught herself how to code. It took quite some time and effort, but once the intention became strong enough, Brittany was determined to make a difference. She kept on trying for months to train her neural network on breast cancer data. And finally, after hundreds of trials, she cracked the code. She subsequently trained her neural network to incorporate 100 troublesome outliers and was so able to greatly improve the program's accuracy. Cloud4Cancer has yet to be approved by the Food and Drug Administration (FDA), but it has been tested in institutions in the USA and Italy.

Inspired by her accomplishment, Brittany has since continued her explorations. She has started to work on identifying predictors of flu immune response. After graduating from Duke University, where she studies Biology, she plans to attend medical school at Mount Sinai in Manhattan. She hopes to continue her big data research as a pediatric oncologist.[7]

Sixto Cancel's Efforts to Assist Vulnerable Youth

To Those Who Suffer

Compassion to those
Who suffer from
The unnecessary plight
Of hunger
As they agonize
Toward a slow, painful death
To which we all are guilty
Because we prefer to waste,
And look the other way
Instead of helping fellow beings
In this life to stay

---

[6] Lyons, G. (April 7, 2017). Meet the Duke Senior Who Created a Cancer-Detecting App in High School. Retrieved from https://studybreaks.com/students/brittany-wenger/
[7] Ibid.

Compassion to those
Who suffer from
The always untimely departure
Of a dear, beloved one
As they drown
In an inaccessible stream
Of emotional rapids
Caused by the flow
Of their tears
And wander in a dark world
Of fretfulness and fears

Compassion to those
Who suffer from
The artificial bounds
Of their own beliefs
As they wallow
In a projected forest
Of shadows and shades
Created by the blinders
Surrounding their mind:
Just as fearful of the future
As the past that now lies behind
　　　　　　　-Joan Marques

Paying attention and acting upon the needs of those who are treated as if they are insignificant is a praiseworthy trait. Sixto Cancel has this trait. He has made some impressive strides in his young life so far to step up and provide a voice to the voiceless. Sixto used his background as a foster child that went through several homes in Connecticut as a reflective inspiration for his actions.[8] He had one important quality that assisted him in making a difference: grit. He was able to review his circumstances as an example of what needed to be improved for foster children in America. Thanks to his resilience and inner strength, and in spite of moving from one unstable family to another, he graduated high school and entered university. His entrepreneurial and activist skills emerged in junior high when he realized that, just like him, most foster children were struggling with their SATs. This led him to initiate "Stellar Works," a project focused on tutoring and assisting kids with similarly challenging backgrounds as his. He even got teachers on board to become

---

[8] Youth Changemaker: Sixto Cancel (2018). Retrieved from https://sparkaction.org/changemaker/youth-changemaker-sixto-cancel.

tutors to the students in need. From support toward SAT, the focus expanded to support in math and reading to foster kids: Sixto managed to obtain funding from the state and from private donors and managed to set up the tutoring campaign needed.[9]

Inspired by his accomplishments, Sixto expanded his operations to assist foster care children and help them find a respectable place in society. He became a major and successful advocate for allowing foster children to visit their siblings. Soon he became a member of organizations involved in care for foster children, a responsibility he accepted with great pride. He successfully pleaded to give foster children who had to move out on their own duffel bags rather than the traditional garbage bags to put their things in, pointing out the degrading subliminal message captured in giving someone a garbage bag to move on with. The campaign was successful in that it brought to light that the state of Connecticut, where Sixto lived, already had a duffel bag policy, but had not been implementing it![10]

The organization that Sixto is best known for is the one he founded in 2014: Think of Us, an initiative dedicated to creating an online library of lesson-based videos to coach youth through the complicated process of growing up and finding their way successfully through early adulthood. Think of Us, to which Sixto serves as CEO, aims to reach its goal by bringing increased awareness of the needs of foster youth in society and finding technology-based ways to help them succeed as they develop toward adulthood.[11] Within Think of Us, Sixto has already accomplished some important advancements, such as designing and running the first White House Foster Care and Technology Hackathon, which resulted in some important outcomes. Some of these are new federal regulations, new funding for tech in foster care, six additional hackathons, local technology initiatives, and a shift in the national conversation about foster care and tech.[12]

Think of Us started in 2014 with a modest grant of 3000 dollars, but has since received support from a number of foundations to a total of $360,000.[13] It is run by young people who guide their foster care peers through several projects. There is, for example, the "Life Skills Tools library," with an interactive video database full of information about a wide range of skills to acquire,

[9] Ibid.

[10] Ibid.

[11] Think of Us: Our Mission. Retrieved from https://www.thinkof-us.org/about-us/

[12] Sixto Cancel. Big Think Edge. Retrieved from https://bigthink.com/experts/sixto-cancel

[13] Jenkins, L. M. (May 25, 2016). The Former Foster Youth Behind the White House's Foster Care Hackathon. *The Chronicle of Social Change*. Retrieved from https://chronicleofsocialchange.org/news-2/youth-led-nonprofit-challenges-tech-child-welfare-work-together

such as how to buy a car or how to get into community college. The ultimate strength of Think of Us is to establish a balance between the foster care system and the way the millennials in this system use technology.[14]

Raj Panjabi's Passion About Saving Lives

Fortunate

I am fortunate
For being here today
And I am aware that I can choose
To compare myself to those
Who live in more abundance
Upon which I might feel down
Or to those
Who are less fortunate
Leaving me with a guilty frown

Instead, I will compare myself
To the person I was before
And rejoice in the fact
That today I have learned more
I realize my fortune
And my purpose to pay it forward
In order for those who come after me
To nurture a similar sense
Of gratitude for the here and now
That we share
And for which we care
                                   –Joan Marques

Converting right intention into right action is what matters most in bringing about actual change. Raj Panjabi, a young man of Indian heritage born in Liberia, understood this need when he co-founded Last Mile Health, a non-profit organization that focuses on saving lives in some of the world's most isolated communities. In his early years, Raj and his family moved to the USA, where he earned a medical degree and a master's degree in Public Health. He returned to Liberia in 2005 as a medical student and founded Last Mile Health in 2007, along with a team of five Liberian civil war survivors and American

---

[14] Ibid.

health workers. Raj and his team started their organization because they felt passionate about the fact that no one should die because they live far from the nearest doctor, clinic, or hospital.[15] Explaining the challenge of healthcare in clear terms, the founding team of Last Mile Health states on their website:

> Illness is universal but access to healthcare is not. Worldwide, more than one billion people go their entire lives without ever seeing a health worker. Due to the combined effects of distance and poverty, people living in remote communities often die needlessly from preventable, treatable diseases like pneumonia, diarrhea, malaria, malnutrition, and complications of childbirth.
>
> In Liberia, where our story begins, roughly 1.2 million people live in isolated communities that are more than an hour's walk from the nearest clinic or hospital.[16]

So, how does Last Mile Health try to save lives in remote areas? It partners with governments to develop networks of community health workers (CHWs). CHWs usually have a middle or high school education and work in their own villages, where they are trained by nurses and medical assistants and receive medicines, which they distribute among their neighbors. CHWs also learn to refer ill people in their communities to local clinics for treatment. Of course, the CHWs, nurses, and medical assistants need to be paid, so Last Mile Health always welcomes financial assistance. In 2017, Raj and his organization received a prize from TED of $1 million to launch a Community Health Academy, a project that will redesign the education of CHWs and leaders for the digital age.

In 2015, Raj was listed as one of the World's 50 Greatest Leaders by Fortune, and, in 2016, he was named one of the TIME 100 Most Influential People in the World. In 2017, the government of Liberia honored Raj Panjabi with the distinction of Knight Commander in the Most Venerable Order of the Pioneers of the Republic of Liberia, one of the nation's highest honors.

The Power of Right Intention

As the cases in this chapter demonstrated, right intention is crucial in bringing about a positive change. Of course you should not leave it at that. Right intention, without any follow-up action, remains a figment of our imagination. Yet, when right intention is powerful, it ignites a passion that compels

---

[15] Last Mile Health: What we do. Retrieved from http://lastmilehealth.org/what-we-do/
[16] Last Mile Health: The Challenge. Retrieved from http://lastmilehealth.org/what-we-do/

toward action. As you may have discovered, none of the individuals discussed in this chapter was born in a wealthy family. They were all confronted with numerous challenges in their lives, just like most of us, but used those challenges to expand their views. They observed, experienced, and contemplated how they could make sure that the problems they witnessed or suffered would not perpetuate. While some of these individuals have already risen to global fame (such as Muhamad Yunus and Raj Panjabi), and others are still on their way (such as Brittany Wenger and Sixto Cancel), all of them had others who assisted them to the next level.

This chapter on right intention also demonstrated the intuitive sequence of the eightfold path:

- For each of the individuals reviewed above, the right intention was a result of their right view: they observed a situation and realized that something had to be done.
- The right intention led to right action in each of the cases described.
- For all of these individuals, the right action led to the creation of an organization or the insight into what will become their future livelihood.
- Inspired by the positive effects of their right action, each of these individuals continued their right efforts.
- Given their fulfilling activities, they also engaged in right mindfulness, as they ensured that what they did would be beneficial to larger communities.
- Thanks to this mindfulness, each of these individuals has continuously been able to exert right concentration.

Today

Today is part
Of tomorrow's good old times
When the unpleasant details
Will have withered away
And the highlights
Will have magnified
On a distant future day...

For such is the work of our mind:
We often perceive the past
Through the pink sunglasses
Of affectionate rumination,
Enriched by knowledge
We lack at the moment,

And polished with experiences
That are still in formation

So, let's celebrate today
Regardless of what it feels like
For its setbacks will have proven
Their value tomorrow
And its joys will have accrued
The aura of past glories
Wrapped in the gentle cloud
Of loving memories
                    –Joan Marques

5

Right Speech

Adelita Leticia Fortunata

She was simple, dressed in rags
Adelita Leticia Fortunata
But she had a special gift
That made her everyone's inamorata

With a gleam in her eyes
Every evening, at seven-o-three,
She would draw them to her side
As she sat under the guanabana tree

And when she started talking
You could hear a pin drop
They would all hold their breath
Until Adelita would stop

She would talk about her feelings
As queen of the stars
And her travels through the universe
From Neptune to Mars

And those who were carrying
The worries of the day
Could feel their stress
Slowly fading away

© Springer Nature Switzerland AG 2019
J. Marques, *Lead with Heart in Mind*, https://doi.org/10.1007/978-3-030-17028-8_5

Adelita's stories helped them see
The essence of their lives
And how easy contentment could be
If only sensing their own drives

She taught them that happiness
Is not captured in physical manifestations
But by cherishing meaningful moments
And maintaining valuable relations

So till today, in their mind, they can see
Every evening, at seven-o-three,
How Adelita Leticia Fortunata
The people's eternal inamorata
Would share her happiness theory
Sitting under the guanabana tree
                                        ~Joan Marques

In these times of massive communications in many diverse ways, and an abundance of social media, it is critical that we fully understand the importance of right speech. There's an old adage that goes, "Sticks and stones may break my bones, but words will never hurt me." It sounds pretty brave, but the truth is that words do have the power to heal or wound in a way that far outlasts physical damage: psychologically. Words can be constructive or destructive and should be uttered with caution.

Engaging in right speech means that you deliberately refrain from saying things that have negative effects on others. It also means that you remain cautious with spreading news of which you are unsure, or of which the contents can be devastating to some.

Practicing right speech means that you attempt to resolve division and disharmony and try to promote or restore unison and harmony. Right speech means that you are telling the truth to your best of abilities, not creating divisiveness by telling different people different things, refraining from cruelty in your speech, and withholding yourself from exaggerating facts, only to make them seem more interesting.

In line with Buddha's teaching, Thomas Bruner suggests for us to ask ourselves the following questions to ensure we're engaging in right speech:

- Is it true? Just because we think, feel, or believe something doesn't make it true. Right speech is asking if what we are about to say is accurate, factual, or objectively verifiable.

- Is it helpful? We often speak for our own benefit. Right speech is asking ourselves whether what we will say is helpful, useful, or beneficial to others.
- Is it timely? We usually speak when we want to speak. Right speech asks whether now is the proper or appropriate time to say what we have to say.
- Is it kind? Sometimes we speak out of anger and frustration. Right speech means we speak with good intent, good will, and compassion for others, even—or especially—when we're angry or frustrated.[1]

In the same vein, William Macaux points out some critical aspects we should cease if we want to engage in right speech. These aspects are:

- Lying – This harms trust in relationships, with others, but also with ourselves. Once we realize that, we may come to the decision to forego such unwholesome behavior, and we may find our actions becoming more courageous.
- Harshness – It is important to know that words can be very harmful, and once they are uttered, they cannot be taken back. Harsh words come from a place of hurt, anger, or feeling offended. Using harsh words says a lot about us.
- Backbiting – Gossiping about others, and even self-serving comparisons, have no place in right speech. We all have a choice about what we discuss, so let us be mindful of our topics.
- Useless Talk – This is a particularly abundant problem in today's society. So many people talk for the sake of talking more than others, without really saying anything sensible. This is a waste of everyone's precious time and is not right speech.[2]

When you listen well, you can better practice right speech, because you are interpreting and considering the other party's words and intentions well and you think deeply on them before responding. It may now be clear how right view and right intention, as well as the other treads of the Eightfold Path, can assist us in performing right speech.

In this chapter, we will highlight the essence and context of right intention and discuss some individuals who have practiced right speech, sometimes at difficult moments in their career.

---

[1] Bruner, T. (July 24, 2017). Leadership and Right Speech. Retrieved from http://brunerstrategies.com/2017/07/24/leadership-right-speech/

[2] Macaux, W. (November 7, 2017). Right Speech and Good Leadership. Retrieved from https://generativityllc.com/blog/2017/11/7/right-speech-good-leadership

Binta Niambi Brown's Truth Telling

What's Best

It takes courage to be honest
It takes courage to be fair
It takes courage to remain authentic
When no one else seems to care

It takes grit to follow your passion
It takes guts to listen to your heart
It takes confidence to move in directions
That others consider less smart

It takes awareness to stay the course
It takes energy to find your zest
But why meekly go with the flow
When you already know what's best?
                                    ~Joan Marques

A woman who has become known for her truth-telling courage is Binta Niambi Brown. She is currently the CEO and cofounder of Fermata Entertainment Ltd. She rose to prominence as a successful professional in law, human rights advocacy, media, and government and then made a 190° shift in focus by establishing a music and entertainment business with a thus far unpracticed business model of focusing on maintaining the artists' rights and funding creative platforms that maximize personal expression and community connection. Her mission-oriented platform, B|G Mouth Records, is vying to become the first statutory and certified B Corp.

Brown is a true octopus, as she finds her way through a brilliant career, yet never loses sight of her humble beginnings. She sticks to her strongest belief, which is that honesty is the best strategy.[3] Early on in her career, Brown was confronted with the dilemma of telling the truth and potentially losing a lucrative contract, or keeping the truth hidden till the deal was sealed. She chose to practice right speech by telling the client of a $3 billion asset acquisition what she knew, thereby risking a major financial setback for herself and

---

[3] Giang, V. (June 6 2015). 7 Business Leaders Share How They Solved the Biggest Moral Dilemmas of Their Careers. Fastcompany.com. Retrieved from http://www.fastcompany.com/3046630/lessons-learned/7-business-leaders-share-how-they-solved-the-biggest-moral-dilemmas-of-their

her business partner. She was well-aware that telling the truth at such a critical moment so early in her career could ruin the deal and be disastrous for her future professional path. She understood well that she was risking major reputation loss among colleagues. However, she decided that she could rather live with that than with concealing the truth to her client. Ultimately, the deal went through, and Brown learned an important lesson that paved the path of her business behavior from there on: honesty is the best strategy.[4]

Yet, there is more to Brown's behavior than mere right speech. Her career choice and performance demonstrate the interconnectedness between various treads of the Eightfold Path. She began dreaming of being a lawyer when she was merely 10 years old, after hearing a congressman telling her class that he knew he wanted to be a politician when he was their age. She realized the improved quality of life her family enjoyed due to the civil rights movement and decided that law was the way for her to contribute further to righteous causes. She was also aware that being a lawyer would enable her to make a positive difference for large groups in the future. Soon after becoming a law firm associate, she realized the glaring lack of women of color in her position and decided to become a fundraiser for political causes, arts organizations, and her alma mater, Barnard College.[5] Binta's determination drove her forth to become one of the top young black fundraisers in the USA. She became highly involved in Hillary Clinton's 2008 presidential campaign and was elected a trustee of Barnard College at age 34. In Brown's just-described actions, we can detect the three treads of the Noble Eightfold Path discussed so far, right views, right intentions, and right speech, as well as the ones to be discussed hereafter, right actions, right livelihood, right efforts, right concentration, and right mindfulness.

Malala Yousafzai and Her Vocal Advocacy for Education

Sparkling Diamond

Distinguished are those
Who ever experienced the agony
Of a heart torn apart

---

[4] Ibid.

[5] Potkewitz, H. (2011). Driven to make justice her business. *Crain's New York Business, 27* (13), F8.

By the loss of something dear

For they have learned
What can only be taught through pain:
Empathy and understanding
And compassion for a tear

The world, to broken-hearted,
Becomes a zone of concordance
In the dark
That connection emanates…

For every crack in one's heart
Adds to the abundance
Of the spark
That this diamond ultimately radiates…
                                        ~Joan Marques

A young, now globally renowned performer of right speech is Malala Yousafzai known for her bold and brave human rights advocacy for education of women and children in her native Swat Valley in northwest Pakistan. Malala has demonstrated that daring to speak the truth holds major risks but also harbors the potential of becoming a global movement and acquiring the ears and respect of the world. In 2014, Yousafzai became the youngest-ever Nobel Peace Prize laureate.

Born in 1997, Malala was confronted with inequality and oppression at an early stage. In her native area, the local Taliban had banned girls from attending school. In 2009, when she was barely 12 years old, Malala started writing a blog under a pseudonym for the BBC Urdu. In this blog, she described her life under Taliban oppression. Her outreach efforts attracted the attention of a New York Times journalist, who made a documentary about Malala's life. This really brought her into the limelight with a wide range of human rights and children organizations but also caught the attention of the Taliban, and in October 2012, while on a bus from school, Malala and two other girls were shot by a Taliban gunman, who was out to assassinate her as punishment for her activism. Malala was shot in the head and remained unconscious for quite some time in the local hospital. When her condition finally started improving, she was transferred to a hospital in the UK. While the assassin may have attempted to take her life, his actions actually brought Malala more prominence than ever before in the world. She was at one point even referred to as potentially the most famous teenager in the world.

As the world denounced the Taliban's actions, this religious organization threatened to increase its efforts to kill Malala as a means of religious justice. Malala stayed in the UK and became a globally renowned voice for the right to education. She started a nonprofit organization and co-authored "I am Malala," which became an international best seller. Since then, she has been the recipient of numerous awards and honors worldwide. Malala's brave advocacy has expanded into an international movement, and Pakistan's Prime Minister, Shahid Khaqan Abbasi, named her "the most prominent citizen" of the country.

In 2013, Malala spoke before the United Nations and had an audience with Queen Elizabeth II in Buckingham Palace. That same year she also spoke at Harvard University and met with then US President Barack Obama and his family. Her education advocacy expanded to a global level, and her efforts led her to travel to many places in the world and enabled her to make a firm donation toward the rebuilding of 65 schools in Gaza. She is the founder of the Malala Fund, which invests in local education initiatives for girls in Pakistan, Afghanistan, Nigeria, Kenya, and Jordan, where it focuses on Syrian refugees. In 2018, Malala returned to Pakistan for the first time since the attack in 2014, in which she almost lost her life. This is particularly a courageous act when considering the mixed feelings about the world's youngest Nobel laureate. While she is revered by many for the awareness she brought globally to education for girls in her home country and several others, there are also many people in Pakistan who consider her a troublemaker who needs to be silenced.

Paul Polman's Bold Stance Toward Shareholders

Big Deal

We make such a big deal of our life
We get enthralled by unending strife
Diligently we aim for a major role
In our rush for power we lose our soul

We confuse affluence with happiness
Our priority-list has turned into a mess
Stress has become a part of our routine:
If we don't tag along, we won't be seen

We dance to a tune we learned so well
The music of "do you know what you sell?"
Because the path to fortune and fame
Is tough and for no two of us the same

And though we get confronted with death
We choose to think we'll have eternal breath
The daily grindstone is all that counts:
Our gains and how our position mounts

But life is short – too soon we find out
Then, we get to wonder what it was all about…

But the lessons we ultimately teach to others
Get lost and remain the least of our bothers
And we find, even before our lifeline breaks
That another one carries on our mistakes…

~Joan Marques

In early 2009, Paul Polman became the new CEO of Unilever, a global consumer product and food corporation, known for brands such as Lipton tea, Ben & Jerry's ice cream, and Vaseline skin care products. The business world was still very much in the clutches of the global financial crisis, and Polman did what very few CEOs dare to do, especially new ones: he notified Unilever's shareholders that they should stop expecting quarterly annual and earnings guidance reports for the stock market. He stressed that the company was now going to take a longer view, and whoever was not happy about that could take their money and invest it somewhere else.[6]

Shortly after making this bold statement, Unilever's share price declined by 8%, because a fear emerged that there was bad news on the horizon in a company that had not done too well in recent history. But Polman, who was the first Unilever CEO in a long time to come in from the external environment rather than internally rising through the ranks (he previously worked at Procter & Gamble and Nestlé), did not stop there. He started disinviting some shareholders, which is quite unheard in business circles, and caused quite an upheaval in the company.[7]

---

[6] Boynton, A. (July 20, 2015). Unilever's Paul Polman: CEOs Can't Be 'Slaves' To Shareholders. Forbes. Retrieved from https://www.forbes.com/sites/andyboynton/2015/07/20/unilevers-paul-polman-ceos-cant-be-slaves-to-shareholders/#53da9874561e
[7] Ibid.

Polman, a major advocate for value creation and sustainable approaches, openly resented shareholders that are only out to get their money multiplied without really caring for the nature and behavior of the business they have invested it in. He affirmed that slavery has been abolished long ago, so shareholders should stop behaving as if they are slave drivers.

During his tenure at Unilever, Paul Polman saw his main responsibility as being to a large group of stakeholders, including consumers from all parts of the world and climate change activists. He took it as his leadership task to double Unilever's revenue while at the same time halving its environmental footprint. To that end, the company established the Unilever Sustainable Living Plan.[8] While he understood that his ambitious goals would not be completely fulfilled during his tenure, he felt that he needed to initiate a change of mindset, which could then be carried on after him.

Polman didn't consider his vocal stance toward shareholders a demonstration of courage. He preferred to call it leadership, but asserted that courage enables you to put others' interests ahead of your own and be willing to take responsible risks. Polman was very much aware that a change toward massive adoption of a sustainable mindset would be a herculean task that would not happen overnight. He was aware that there would be many opponents and skeptics that would try to impede any effort toward doing the right thing in business. And indeed, he experienced opposition from companies that benefitted from keeping things as they were, such as the carbon-based industry. Yet, he considered every opposition an opportunity for future collaboration.[9]

Paul Polman, who announced in November 2018 that he would step down as chief executive officer of Unilever, particularly criticized Milton Friedman's teachings about the purpose of business to be self-serving and make profit and do so without any further regard for the environment. He has always been an advocate for longer-term thinking and continues to maintain a solid realization that business has a supporting function in the global economy, a need which he felt manifested itself clearly in the 2008 global financial crisis. Polman continues to believe in serving: in helping those that cannot help themselves. Among the many issues the world struggles with today are inequality, poverty, youth unemployment, and climate change; Polman believes that everyone—business included—should play a role in addressing them. So, aside from tending to environmental concerns, he focused Unilever's operations on livelihoods and social compliance. He was concerned about the

---

[8] Sustainable Living. Unilever website. Retrieved from https://www.unilever.com/sustainable-living/

[9] Boynton, A. (July 20, 2015). Unilever's Paul Polman: CEOs Can't Be 'Slaves' To Shareholders. *Forbes*. Retrieved from https://www.forbes.com/sites/andyboynton/2015/07/20/unilevers-paul-polman-ceos-cant-be-slaves-to-shareholders/#53da9874561e

large numbers of young people who are unemployed or hold marginal jobs in the world. He increased Unilever's sustainable sourcing from 10% in 2009 to 60%, but admitted during his leadership tenure that the company still has a long way to go.

In order to expand the circle of awareness, Polman engaged in a lot of networks, many of them consisting of young people and social entrepreneurs. This is how he encountered creative ideas and positive engagement, as well as hope that the world is getting closer to an overall awareness that we have to change our thought patterns toward more sustainable living.[10] Polman also serves as chairman of the World Business Council for Sustainable Development, member of the International Business Council of the World Economic Forum, and member of the B Team and serves on the Board of the UN Global Compact and the Consumer Goods Forum, where he co-chairs the Sustainability Committee.[11]

Polman's efforts have been noticed by attentive and sustainability conscious sources. In 2017, he was recognized as one of the inaugural "Heroes of Conscious Capitalism" at the annual CEO Summit along with 27 other business leaders.[12] He was recognized for his contribution toward realizing a world in which business is both practiced and recognized as a force for good.

Ehren Watada's Moral Refusal

It's all about Walking

It's all about walking, one step at the time
Through life, through the day…a never ending rhyme
The road is uneven- here winding, there straight
Bumpy if you're impatient, but smoother if you wait

It's all about walking, one step at the time
On days worth a dollar, and on days worth a dime
Work is important, but even more is happiness
So do what you like to; don't settle for any less

It's all about walking, one step at the time
No need for a hurry, you're now in your prime

---

[10] Ibid.

[11] Shawbel, D. (Nov 1, 2017). Unilever's Paul Polman: Why Today's Leaders Need To Commit To A Purpose. Forbes. Retrieved from https://www.forbes.com/sites/danschawbel/2017/11/21/paul-polman-why-todays-leaders-need-to-commit-to-a-purpose/#32fb65411276

[12] Ibid.

Enjoy every flower, make time for some love
The stroll is soon over, time flies like a dove

It's all about walking, one step at the time
An act with some talking, but more so with mime
Long seem the rainy days, short shines the sun
Easy feels the stroll, exhausting the run

It's all about walking, one step at the time
The art is to stay clean, unspoiled by life's grime
And though falling's easy – for slippery's the trail
The art is to keep standing up- until you set sail.
~Joan Marques

In June 2006, Ehren Watada found himself placed before a monumental moral dilemma. He had joined the Army after the war in Iraq had begun and had served 1 year in South Korea, to be subsequently assigned to Fort Lewis, Washington. A First Lieutenant of the US Army at the time, Watada soon learned that his unit would be deploying to Iraq. In preparation for this to happen, he started doing research about Iraq, its culture, and the reasons for the US involvement in this country.

His in-depth readings of books and articles, along with interviews with veterans who had returned from Iraq, provided him a view that turned out to be less desirable by his employer, the US Army: Watada felt that the reasons for a war in Iraq were illegal and unjust, so, early in 2006, he tried to submit his resignation, stating that he was genuinely opposed to the war in Iraq and referring to this war as lawless and dishonest. He therefore felt that participating in this particular war would make him an accomplice to war crimes: something he abhorred. He underscored that his opposition was not against every war. Just this one. To prove his point, he offered to serve in Afghanistan instead. However, that was refused, and he was offered a desk job in Iraq, which he in turn refused.

As a result of his refusal to serve as ordered, the Army prepared a court-martial process, with the possibility of Watada serving up to 7 years in prison, along with dismissal from service. In spite of the pending punishment, Watada stood by his decision, because he felt that it was a morally responsible one. He explained that he did not want to regret his actions when he would tell his children in the future how he lived his life, nor did he want to look back on a life of mindless actions and immoral decisions.

Once the charges were presented, it turned out that the Army made it a point to not only try to penalize Watada for his refusal to serve in Iraq but also for his vocal criticism of the Army in the media. By doing this, the Army aimed to send out a strong message to others in military service that criticizing a war or any decision made to lead the nation into war could lead to severe penalties.

In court, the Army prosecutor labeled Watada's actions as condescending to the President and contended that Watada's public announcements were destructive to the morale in his unit. The most important focus of the Army in this case, it seemed, was to use Watada as an example for future occurrences, thus discouraging military personnel from criticizing decisions made by the Army. In court, several parties were heard from both sides: individuals from academia, from the military, and from other civilian disciplines, who categorically labeled the war in Iraq as unlawful and immoral, but also military personnel that expressed concern about Watada's stance and approach to his employer. In the end, Watada was court-martialed in February 2007, with the case ending in a mistrial.[13]

He had faced three specifications, one for missing movement (refusal to participate in the war in Iraq) and two for "conduct unbecoming an officer and a gentleman," pertaining to Watada's public comments criticizing his employer (the President of the USA) and the war.

The judge ultimately ruled that the court-martial was unable to decide the question of whether the deployment order was unlawful and decided to strike Watada's stipulation, calling it an admission of guilt. The judge subsequently granted the request for a mistrial.

The Army did not leave matters as decided by the judge and scheduled a new court-martial, which was postponed several times, due to Watada's defense attorney's claim of double jeopardy. Yet, the Army challenged this, stating that a mistrial is not a decision. Watada's defense refuted that the jeopardy was attached to the presentation of evidence, leading to the mistrial. The District Judge, Benjamin Settle, therefore declared Lt. Watada's double jeopardy claim valid. Upon this ruling, the Army went into higher appeal, but at that time the Obama administration had taken office, and the Justice Department asked the court to drop the case.

Two years later, in 2009, the Army discharged Watada under "Other-Than-Honorable" (OTH) conditions, which is the least favorable type of Army administrative discharge. While the OTH discharge was not what Watada would have wanted, he expressed his gratitude that matters did not end in prison term or worse.[14]

Throughout the case, Ehren Watada received strong response, both positive and negative, from many sides, individually and organizationally. Celebrities such as Sean Penn, Jane Fonda, and Tim Robbins and organizations such as

---

[13] *Court Martial of Lt. Ehren Watada Ends with A Surprise. Hawaii News Now.* Retrieved from http://www.hawaiinewsnow.com/story/6055734/court-martial-of-lt-ehren-watada-ends-with-a-surprise-conclusion

[14] The Associated Press (26 Sept 2009). Army Officer Who Refused Iraq Duty Is Allowed to Resign. *New York Times.* Retrieved from https://www.nytimes.com/2009/09/27/us/27discharge.html

the ACLU, Iraq Veterans against the War, and Veterans for Peace were very vocal in that regard. Amnesty International even issued a statement that, in case Watada would be convicted, he would be considered a prisoner of conscience. On the other hand, several Japanese American veterans felt that Watada, as a member of their ethnic and cultural group, had shamed them with his actions.[15] Yet, throughout the upheaval that lasted several years, Watada maintained his stance and ultimately found peace in his life after the discharge. He currently co-owns a restaurant in Las Vegas.

The Courage of Right Speech

It takes courage to engage in right speech. A lot of courage. There are undoubtedly examples you can think of, in which you kept quiet or said something you did not really agree with, because the risk of saying what you considered right might result in too great of a loss. Especially when your livelihood depends on it, you may refrain from right speech. Right speech demands a sense of justice that is greater than the fear that comes with it. If we consider the four individuals discussed in this chapter, we can see some interesting common threads: they all believed in their reason for engaging in right speech, they all knew there was a risk involved, and they all decided that they were going to accept the consequences.

Of the four examples in this chapter, Malala has thus far suffered the largest retaliation effects, while Binta Niambi Brown was fortunate enough that her right speech was appreciated in the end, and even rewarded. In the case of Paul Polman, he also walked the fine line of alienating shareholders and risking his job, but thus far, things have been looking decent for Polman. Ehren Watada suffered years of insecurity and pending punishment of a body that does not condone any retort from followers. While he finally could resign under less favorable conditions, he escaped a prison sentence.

Each of the individuals discussed in this chapter demonstrated heroism by doing what the majority in their position don't do. As courageous loners they stood up against a larger body and spoke their opinion, driven by a deep-rooted sense of conscience. For each of these individuals, it becomes clear that they engaged in right view, felt the urge to display their right intention, and therefore engaged in right speech driven by a quest to perform right action, earn a livelihood for themselves and their loved ones in a rightful way, engage in right effort, practice right mindfulness, and be driven by right concentration.

May we all work up the courage to engage in right speech and its intertwined behaviors.

---

[15] Ibid.

6

Right Action

True Miracles

Although we have a tendency
To consider only the extraordinary
As miracles to be stored
We should all realize by now
What we can't possibly disavow
What just can't be ignored…

True miracles are all around
And can so easily be found
In the smallest things we share:
A smiling child, a helping hand
A mind that wants to understand
The gift of love and care

A true and honest miracle
Makes giver and grantee lyrical
And ignites a glow of grace
It may seem short-lived or fickle
But it will definitely tickle
A smile to every face

The greatest miracle of all
Is that, no matter how small,
We can all be miracle creators

© Springer Nature Switzerland AG 2019
J. Marques, *Lead with Heart in Mind*, https://doi.org/10.1007/978-3-030-17028-8_6

By contributing good intentions
And adding positive dimensions
Through becoming love incubators
            −Joan Marques

Right action starts, interestingly enough, with the discontinuation of the action of harming ourselves and others. Right action could be broadly interpreted, and it requires a careful examination of our behavior. Right action encompasses the protection of life and the preservation of well-being of all living creatures in the broadest sense possible. In Buddhist circles, right action consists of three main considerations: no killing, no stealing, no sexual misconduct. Looking deeper into this, it really means no killing (of any living being), no stealing, no insulting, no lying, no cheating, no backbiting, no harsh words, no manipulating, no mean-spirited thoughts or behavior, and not engaging in any type of misconduct.

Because we are continuously caught in all sorts of situations, it is not always easy to engage in right action, especially when we consider that right action is, in many cases, a personal judgment. Let's zoom into the subject of killing as an example. Killing is an extremely broad topic, because it doesn't only pertain to one person killing another. Killing also entails the practice of killing for pleasure, which often happens when people hunt or fish, and many people become uncomfortable when we get to that aspect of killing. Yet, if we consider that all life is precious, not just our own, and not just the lives of humans, then this mindset makes a lot of sense! Right action is more critical in our times, because our collective wrong actions have led to massive problems such as global warming, and the extinction and destruction of many innocent lives due to inconsiderate behavior.

Humanity, as a whole, has progressed in many ways, but all too often this progress happened at the expense of other beings. Today, the imbalance in income is greater than ever, which means that some pay for the prosperity of others. Human beings and animals in many parts of the world are victimized on a daily basis by those who have become accustomed to extracting and killing what they consider resources for their business or pleasure-based purposes. The immense destruction of natural resources in our few global rainforests without proper replenishment, for instance, has demanded its toll, and since we are not living on an island, we will all ultimately feel the negative effects of these mindless actions.

Ray Anderson's Green Efforts

Nothing New

We're born with 'possessing' as our aim
Because we were given a bodily frame
Which we've come to cherish and adore
As if that's who we are, and nothing more
So, our life becomes an enduring stride
Of chasing possessions, people, and pride
We accumulate anything to make us feel
That the 'physical self' illusion is real
And most of us are devoted to this trend
Until the day comes that it all has to end
The day that we have to give up the stride
Thus, all the possessions, people, and pride
And then we have to surrender the body too
It's an old, recurring story. Nothing new.

~Joan Marques

An American Business leader who discovered the path to right action at a later stage in his professional life is Ray Anderson. In 1973 he founded Interface, a company that would grow out to become the world's largest carpet tile provider. Little did he know, or even care at that time, that he would once be called "the greenest chief executive in America" and receive numerous awards for being a model environmentally conscious leader.[1] In the first two decades of its existence, Interface was highly profit oriented. Yes, Anderson complied with the legal prescriptions of corporate performance, but, as was customary in those days, was not really concerned about the environmental effects of his corporation's activities.

It all changed, however, when in 1994, a team of co-workers started forwarding him questions from customers about Interface's environmental vision, which was completely absent at that time. As Anderson got confronted with these probing questions, he got confronted with a series of books, such as Paul Hawken's *The Ecology of Commerce* and Daniel Quinn's *Ishmael* about humanity's destructive effects on planet Earth, and they provoked a complete paradigm shift within Anderson. Anderson realized the immense crime so

---

[1] *$5 million commitment names Ray C. Anderson Center for Sustainable Business* (January 30, 2015). *Georgia Tech News Center*. Retrieved from http://www.news.gatech.edu/2015/01/30/5-million-commitment-names-ray-c-anderson-center-sustainable-business

many businesses commit to our environment without being punished and decided to become the change he wanted to see in the world. He started his mission of making carpets sustainably, something that only gradually transformed from a prior "impossibility" to an achievable dream, because carpet production, by default, is highly destructive to the environment.[2]

For the next 17 years, Anderson operated on many fronts to enhance awareness for environmental sustainability: he worked internally, with his coworkers and his suppliers, but also externally, through presentations, books, and articles, to encourage other CEOs in doing the same. He got encouraged to do all this after reading that the same source that caused the destruction through a "take-make-waste" approach (business) could also be the initiator of a restoration of the crisis in the biosphere.[3] The internal project toward increased environmental respect was implemented by a task force and called "Climbing Mount Sustainability." The plan consisted of seven focus points: (1) eliminating waste; (2) eliminating toxic substances from products, vehicles, and facilities; (3) operating facilities with renewable energy; (4) redesigning processes and products to solidify a more responsible production cycle; (5) enhancing efficiency to reduce waste and emissions; (6) creating a culture that integrates sustainable principles and engage all stakeholders therein; and (7) creating a new business model that demonstrates and supports the value of sustainability based commerce.[4]

Through the ups and downs in the sustainability journey, Interface has managed to move from using less than 1% of its raw materials from recycled and renewable sources to 49%.[5] Not all efforts were rewarded. Some processes, which initially seemed exciting and progressive, turned out to be mere enlargers of the company's environmental footprint and had to be discontinued. Similarly, some miracles surfaced, of which the Interface team had never expected to see the light. One year before his passing, Anderson wrote a reflection on the role of businesses and industries in environmental sustainability, in which he related the achievements of Interface Inc. for the zero environmental footprint goal. At that time, Interface had decreased greenhouse gas emission by 44% and cut water use by 80%. Anderson strongly believed that

[2] Langer, E. (August 10, 2011). Ray Anderson, "greenest CEO in America," dies at 77. *The Washington Post* Obituaries. Retrieved from http://www.washingtonpost.com/local/obituaries/ray-anderson-greenest-ceo-in-america-dies-at-77/2011/08/10/gIQAGoTU7I_story.html

[3] Anderson, R. (2007). *Doing Well by Doing Good*, in Church, D. (Ed.), *Einstein's Business: Engaging Soul, imagination, and Excellence in the Workplace*. Elite Books, Santa Rosa, CA.

[4] Ibid.

[5] Davis, M. (September 3, 2014). Radical Industrialists: 20 years later, Interface looks back on Ray Anderson's legacy. *Greenbiz.com*. Retrieved from http://www.greenbiz.com/blog/2014/09/03/20-years-later-interface-looks-back-ray-andersons-legacy

business is the major cause and solution for environmental degradation. In his article, Anderson asserted that he would be one of the business people who would continue to exert efforts for sustainability.[6]

Ray Anderson passed away in 2011, but Interface's mission to become fully sustainable by 2020 is still fully in progress. Anderson's incessant efforts to raise awareness on CSR during the last two decades of his life have not gone unnoticed. In 2013, 2 years after his passing, the US Green Building Council (USGBC) instated the annual Radical Industrialism Award in 2013 in honor of Ray Anderson, for having been a corporate sustainability pioneer who was influential in the development of LEED green building certification. The award is sponsored by the Ray C. Anderson Foundation and is granted each year to a leader in the manufacturing sector whose commitment to and achievements in sustainability exemplify Ray's vision, integrating sustainability into the very heart of their company.[7]

Jeremiah Kimbugwe's Health-Conscious Initiative

Life is Yours...

Have you ever wondered about sitting on a cloud?
Drifting over countries and seas,
looking down on mountains and trees...

Have you ever lain on your back in the sand?
Watching the sky above...
feeling nothing but pure, deep love...

Have you ever pictured being the highest branch in a tree?
Waving in the wind...
proud, high and distinct...

Have you ever cherished a scent that was unique?
Burning sand on a plain...
hot asphalt in the rain...

---

[6] Anderson, R. C. (2010, April). Earth Day, Then and Now. Sustainability: *The Journal of Record*. pp. 73–74.
[7] Colgate-Palmolive (November 30, 2015). Colgate-Palmolive Receives Sustainability Leadership Award at 2015 Greenbuild Conference. *Business Wire* (English).

Are you still looking under trees and between leaves?
For gnomes in red and white,
and elves, feather light…

Are you often finding your eyes…
Searching the sky…
for UFO's flying by…

Are you allowing yourself to dream
No matter how hard life may sometimes seem?

Keep the child within you alive…
It's the secret behind every drive.

This life is yours my friend…
Enjoy it till the end.

~Joan Marques

A splendid example of a young leader living "right action" is Jeremiah Kimbugwe, who is only 25 years old at the time of writing this chapter (2018) but is already involved in several constructive projects in his home country, Uganda. Jeremiah is a social worker who holds a degree in Social Development and focuses on bringing about healthy changes and works with Sovhen Uganda, a registered national non-governmental organization that operates in the slums of Kampala City and other remote areas in Uganda. His aim is to lead positive transformation among the youth with the intention of bringing about a peaceful, united, and healthy world. In his own words:

> As a recent graduate, I joined the cause to lead positive transformation in my fellow youth with the intention of bringing about a peaceful, united and healthy world—one that offers marginalized children and youth an opportunity to have a say and be involved in the socio-economic development decisions that are affecting them.[8]

Uganda faces a number of problems related to inadequate healthcare, education, and economic opportunity. There are many needs, but there are also young members such as Jeremiah in the community, who demonstrate great potential, resilience, and creativity toward bringing progress.[9] When he was

---

[8] Kimbugwe, J. (December 12, 2017). Helping Out in my Home Country. *The Huffington Post.* Retrieved from https://www.huffingtonpost.com/kimbugwe-jeremiah/post_3309_b_1475859.html
[9] Jeremiah Kimbugwe. Retrieved from https://www.huffingtonpost.com/author/kimbugwe-jeremiah

only 17, Jeremiah volunteered with World Vision Uganda, serving there as a child sponsorship assistant. This may be where some important seeds were planted, because even when he was enrolled in University, he decided to mobilize his friends toward creating an association that rapidly flourished into a nonprofit organization with international membership. He represented the organization in a youth-to-youth fund competition organized by the International Labor Organization (ILO). Thanks to his compelling story, Jeremiah emerged as the best among 400 participating nonprofits.[10]

One of the projects Jeremiah oversees is a sanitary napkin-making project, which is a solution to dangerous and unsanitary circumstances for young women in his home country. The sanitary napkins are made from local materials and are environmentally friendly, as a way to protect and conserve nature. With this project, Jeremiah focuses on girls' education and income generation, because the availability of sanitary pads improves female school attendance, combats high dropout rates, and provides employment opportunities for local women. Jeremiah is aware that keeping girls in school is crucial for the future strength of the country. The jobs Jeremiah's organization creates not only generate income but also focus on training the women to be entrepreneurs themselves.[11]

Another project that Jeremiah is passionate about is a community-based health center, created to combat the high spread of malaria in his community. Each of these projects aims at producing affordable items while at the same time creating employment opportunities for the young mothers and helping the young girls to stay in school. A third project that Jeremiah is involved in is a business development project run by volunteers and aimed at providing business training to young people.[12] Several of the trainees from this program have since started up businesses or improved on the ventures they had before. Jeremiah sees this as a sign of development in his career and an inspiration to continue advocating for entrepreneurship in the communities he serves.

Creative as they are, Jeremiah and his team came up with a program they titled SEED: Saving for Education, Entrepreneurship and Down Payment. Schoolchildren receive small boxes with numbers and run small projects at home with the help of their parents in order to save for their basic educational needs. Jeremiah asserts:

---

[10] Kimbugwe, J. (December 12, 2017). Helping Out in my Home Country. *The Huffington Post*. Retrieved from https://www.huffingtonpost.com/kimbugwe-jeremiah/post_3309_b_1475859.html

[11] Jeremiah Kimbugwe. Retrieved from https://www.huffingtonpost.com/author/kimbugwe-jeremiah

[12] Jeremiah Kimbugwe. Retrieved from https://www.oneyoungworld.com/profile-main/19872

Just as I have always told my friends, opportunities will come and knock on our doors, and if we are not prepared, they will pass us by. The opportunities will knock on the doors of other people until they find someone who is ready for the challenge.[13]

Jeremiah's projects are all based on his conviction that capacity-building is the core of successful development. He wants to encourage Ugandans, give them a voice, and allow their energy to work toward a better future. With small steps, humility, and a strong belief in his peers, Jeremiah believes that he is starting to build stronger, more stable communities.[14]

Kenton Lee's Shoes that Grow

Happiness

Happiness is not for sale
It is not tied to specifics
Such as our job, our relationships
Or even our living quarters
It is not tied to our bank account
Our education level
Or our status in society
And it doesn't just ease into our soul
On a sunny summer morning
During a quiet stroll

Happiness lies within
It is the realization that everything
Happens at the right time
And that, in retrospect,
Even the most incomprehensible act
Will turn out to make perfect sense
It is gratitude for all we are
Contentment with our life today
And understanding that this moment
Is what it should be anyway

---

[13] Kimbugwe, J. (December 12, 2017). Helping Out in my Home Country. *The Huffington Post*. Retrieved from https://www.huffingtonpost.com/kimbugwe-jeremiah/post_3309_b_1475859.html

[14] Jeremiah Kimbugwe. Retrieved from https://www.huffingtonpost.com/author/kimbugwe-jeremiah

Yet, happiness can be a challenge
If we consider that every 3.6 seconds
A person dies from starvation
If we realize how many living beings
Are abused and killed every day
As a result of our mass ignorance
Should we look away?
Should we just forget?
Does happiness mean: I don't care
If it seems a bit far from my bed?
                    ~Joan Marques

It was during his 2007 work experience at an orphanage in Kenya that pastor Kenton Lee got his epiphany toward a mega right action: he saw a little girl walking with shoes that were far too small for her. However, her parents could not afford newer or larger ones. Looking further, he discovered that many children in the village where he worked were either walking around barefooted or with shoes that had long ago seen their best times. This was particularly concerning when considering the dirt and disease to which so many children's feet get exposed when they walk around barefooted or with shoes that are broken in mountainous areas, grassland, or swamps for hours at a time.

The image of the little girl with shoes too small for her feet lingered in Lee's mind, and when he returned to his hometown in Idaho, he started developing his idea to make a shoe that would grow over time, so that a child could wear it for many years without problems. He pitched an early concept of "the shoe that grows" to several shoe companies among which Nike and Adidas, but none of them were interested.[15] Yet, this did not dishearten Lee, and he assembled a small team with which he continued to work on prototypes. The team worked together with an Oregon-based shoe design studio called Proof of Concept and focused on three main qualities: this shoe had to (1) grow as much as possible, (2) last as long as possible, and (3) cost as little as possible.[16] It took them 5 years of self-study and exploration before "the shoe that grows" came into being, but once it was, it guaranteed five shoe sizes in one and represented an ingeniously simple solution: a pair of sandals that expand as easily as a belt![17] The "shoe that grows" has three areas where it can expand: the

---

[15] The shoe that grows: Our story begins in Nairobi, Kenya in 2007… Retrieved from https://theshoethatgrows.org/about-us/
[16] Wilson, M. (May 22, 2015). For Just $12, These Shoes Will Grow With Your Kid. *FastCompany*. Retrieved from https://www.fastcompany.com/3046506/for-just-12-these-shoes-will-grow-with-your-kid
[17] Ibid.

front, which is adjustable; the sides which come with snaps to allow a wider width; and the back which is fitted with a strap.[18] The upper is made of notched leather, sort of like a pair of Birkenstocks with snaps. The sole made of durable pressed rubber, similar to tires. The shoes are made in two sizes, small and large, the small being suitable from kindergarten to fourth grade and the large lasting from fifth grade through ninth.[19] With his "shoe that grows," Kenton Lee's main idea was to guarantee greater and longer safety for kids in poorer parts of the world.

Once the model was prepared, Kenton and his team created a nonprofit, Because International, and started raising funds to be able to make a large number of these shoes and donate them to kids in need. At the time of writing this chapter, he had donated 100,000 pairs of shoes to children in 89 countries.[20]

The Shoe that Grows is different from Tom's Shoes in many ways: it is more durable, expands and can therefore be worn for a long time, and is offered at a lower price ($15), which makes donation more attractive. And it is donated in large quantities to countries such as Mexico, Malawi, India, and Cambodia.[21]

Much to his surprise, there turned out to be interest for "the shoe that grows" in the USA as well! Yet, even though these shoes are of durable quality, Lee and his organization are aware that the marketing influences to which youngsters in the USA are exposed will soon drive them to exchange their shoes for different, more fashionable ones, even when they are still perfectly wearable.

Today, Kenton Lee is not only the founder of "the shoe that grows," but he also serves as a sought-after public speaker, who encourages young people to explore their social entrepreneurial skills to make the world a better place, even though they may not think they are capable of doing so. He emphasizes on small things that make a big difference and has his story, as well as some other examples, to use as illustration. Most importantly he emphasizes that you don't have to have a super-high level of education to make a powerful difference.[22]

---

[18] Chhabra, E. (June 30, 2015). The Shoe That Keeps On Growing: Finding Solutions to Everyday Problems. *Forbes*. Retrieved from https://www.forbes.com/sites/eshachhabra/2015/06/30/the-shoe-that-keeps-on-growing-finding-solutions-to-everyday-problems/#38478d4a7cb1

[19] Wilson, M. (May 22, 2015). For Just $12, These Shoes Will Grow With Your Kid. *FastCompany*. Retrieved from https://www.fastcompany.com/3046506/for-just-12-these-shoes-will-grow-with-your-kid

[20] *Rave Speakers: Kenton Lee*. Retrieved from https://www.ravespeakers.com/kenton-lee/

[21] Chhabra, E. (June 30, 2015). The Shoe That Keeps On Growing: Finding Solutions to Everyday Problems. *Forbes*. Retrieved from https://www.forbes.com/sites/eshachhabra/2015/06/30/the-shoe-that-keeps-on-growing-finding-solutions-to-everyday-problems/#38478d4a7cb1

[22] *Rave Speakers: Kenton Lee*. Retrieved from https://www.ravespeakers.com/kenton-lee/

Arpit Dhupar's Solution to Pollution

Frown

Disparity is the bitter seed
That has overrun our world
As an obstinate, indestructible weed
Fertilized by the mentality
Of the most despotic ruler
One could come across:
Humanity

Tolerated by a society
Trapped in a devious narrative
Nurtured and Unchallenged
Rationalizing this repulsive nonsense
As if it were the only truth
Unbreakable and unmistakable:
Insanity

Supremacy versus inferiority
Wealth versus poverty
Privilege versus deprivation
Abundance versus starvation:
Our collective reality
Conveniently maintained…
Mundanity!
                    ~Joan Marques

Arpit Dhupar is a mechanical engineer who believes, as he states on his LinkedIn page, that every innovation has to be backed up with a strong business plan in order to reach masses. He adds that technology can be a major instrument in overcoming some of the direst challenges society currently faces. He is also a firm believer that the world's biggest problems can be solved by relatively simple technologies.

Dhupar earned his degree as a mechanical engineer in 2014 and has been diligently working since to improve the lives of people. One of his college projects was the creation of an agriculture machine that could reduce urea consumption in rice fields by 40% and increase yield by 25. Based on his ongoing efforts, Arpit has won various awards from the American Society of Mechanical Engineers, the Department of Science and Technology, Lockheed Martin, FICCI, and others.

Arpit is passionate about research and development and works on multiple projects that will contribute to society's well-being and can improve the quality of life for many. His interest is mainly geared toward renewable energy, pollution reduction devices, and farm mechanization.

Arpit Dhupar is a great example of an individual who converted bad experiences in his life to virtues. Having been brought up in the city of Delhi, he was diagnosed at a young age with a condition that prevented him from playing sports. The condition turned out to be a result from the poor air quality and enormous pollution that troubles so many parts of India, which is home to 14 of the world's 15 most polluted cities, according to the World Health Organization (WHO). Indian people are subject to some of the worst air pollution in the world, with smog levels often soaring during the scorching summers, when heavy, smoke-emanating diesel generators are used to offset power shortages.[23]

As Arpit grew up and had the opportunity to study, he chose to become an engineer, fixated on solving the problem of pollution. His plan was to eliminate pollution from combustion of fossil fuels. By doing this, he wanted to enable access to clean air by using technology to convert pollution to ink and paints.

Along with Kushagra Srivastava, Arpit founded Chakr Innovation, and they developed the world's first continuous self-cleaning trap for particulate matter emissions from the combustion of fossil fuels. This is a major step in development, since more than 7 million premature deaths are linked to air pollution every year, with over 1.1 million deaths in India alone.[24] The innovative technology that Chakr Foundation created can reduce fossil fuel emissions by more than 80%. But the story doesn't end there! The captured pollution is collected in a tank and converted into inks, so that the disposal of the pollutants happens in the most environmentally benign way.[25] The ink can then be used for printing on T-Shirts, banners, mugs, and other promotional items. By creating this constructive cycle and eliminating a destructive one, Chakr has enabled individuals and organizations to help create a sustainable world.[26]

The device that Arpit and his growing team of more than 18 engineers have created needs to be attached to generators in order to capture up to 90% of soot particles from cooled diesel exhaust. The converted material can be sold

---

[23] In polluted India, engineers find novel way to fight diesel exhaust (June 6, 2018). The Economic Times – REUTERS. Retrieved from https://in.reuters.com/article/health-india-pollution-ink/in-polluted-india-engineers-find-novel-way-to-fight-diesel-exhaust-idINKCN1J20HE

[24] Arpit Dhupar. Echoing Green. Retrieved from https://www.echoinggreen.org/fellows/arpit-dhupar

[25] Ibid.

[26] Ibid.

to ink manufacturers. So far, Chakr Innovation has installed more than 50 devices in government firms and offices, saving 1500 billion liters of air from pollution. Meanwhile, Dhupar and his team have raised over $1.5 million in the form of equity funding and grants.[27] Yet, expansion in funding and implementation of this project is needed, particularly in light of the fact that the Indian government intends to erect about 109 smart cities in India, which will trigger increased urbanization, and thus, augmented pollution! Greenpeace India published a report titled "Airpocalypse" in which they state that diesel generators are the biggest culprit in the case of air pollution.

The Fulfillment of Right Action

As you may have noticed in this chapter, right action is not always easy, especially in the initiation stage, but it is very rewarding once the first steps on the path are set. In order to engage in right action, you will have to contemplate deeply on as many aspects of your action as possible. Sometimes you may think you engage in right action, but overlook the effect it may have on large groups of people or other living beings, whom you simply forgot to consider. For example, a project developer may think he is bringing development and employment in a country or state, but underestimate the ecological disruption and the destruction of valuable natural habitat. By not taking all factors in consideration, an act that initially feels like right action may soon become a nightmare to many, and the "actors" may end up being condemned rather than praised!

This underscores once again that all elements of the noble eightfold path should be practiced collaboratively. When engaging in right action, you should make sure this is in line with a right view, which you should verify through communication with those you respect and who can help you see other angles. With right action, you should also make sure it is based on right intention. You don't want your right action to just be a lucky turn for the best. The foundational mindset is critical in working out and implementing a plan. And then there is right speech, which is important in right action, because you will have to walk your talk and talk your walk: you will have to communicate to stakeholders, large and small, direct and indirect, what your course of action will be and how you envision this to benefit all constituents. Also,

---

[27] Mannan, L. (20 Dec. 2017). Recycling pollution: Chakr Innovation is converting diesel soot into ink and paints. *Your Story*. Retrieved from https://yourstory.com/2017/12/recycling-pollution-chakr-innovation-is-converting-diesel-soot-into-ink-and-paints/

when you engage in right action, make sure it remains in line with right livelihood. Some people may frown on this and wonder: would it ever be possible to engage in right action and still practice wrong livelihood? Well, of course! There have been, through time, many people who stole from the rich to give to the poor. In their mind that was justified, but it was still stealing, regardless whom it happened from. So, keep the right livelihood part in scope closely. And then, right effort: this could be seen as the immediate predecessor to right action: only if you engage in right effort will you produce right action. Of course there is always a slight chance that right effort backfires, and the same goes for right intention. Yet, your chance for better overall success is greater if you make sure your intention, effort, and action are well-aligned. Right mindfulness is critical in right action, because the mind is the continuous guide throughout our behavioral patterns. Right mindfulness will keep you atop any possible setbacks and challenges that may emerge, as it guarantees a heightened level of wakefulness throughout your days. Right concentration, which could be seen as the twin of right mindfulness, will assist in maintaining stronger focus on the essence of the action. A possible way to explain their synergy is that right concentration will ensure the fulfillment of the action, while right mindfulness will ensure the fulfillment of the rightfulness of the action.

A powerful way of considering the importance of right action is to take one more look at the leaders described in this chapter:

- Ray Anderson had already made a name for himself by founding and managing one of the first carpet tile factories in the USA, but when he decided to engage in right action and minimize his carbon footprint, and help other business leaders also engage in right action, he secured a much stronger legacy and made his company a much more appreciated part of society than ever before.
- Jeremiah Kimbugwe may have become a successful activist or even project developer and implementer in his home country, but the question remains if he would have received so much appreciation if he were only interested in making money? By starting a project that solves a major underlying problem in his country and creates a revolutionary trend, he is not only feeling much better about his purpose in life but can rest assured that his project will make a positive difference for decades to come in the entire region.
- Kenton Lee could have gone the exact way as Tom's Shoes did and become famous among numerous people who fail to scrutinize the real action behind a so-called good deed. Yet, Kenton wanted to make a long-lasting

difference at an affordable prize and worked on creating this shoe that grows, which has since brought him more appreciation and recognition than he ever envisioned.

- Arpit Dhupar could have only focused on the pollution reduction of his device, but instead gave the entire project an even more positive spin by also supporting an entirely different industry: promotional materials, based on the conversion of pollution into ink. By converting bad experiences to virtues, he made many more people happy and provided even more with a secure livelihood at little cost.

7

Right Livelihood

Avoid Future Pain

Feeble, fickle, and frail
Is the path we tread
When we seek our passion
In earning our daily bread

Finding meaning and purpose
While generating our monthly pay
Considering the effects of our actions
In a future – far beyond today

There's so much to reflect on
In defining a truly rewarding mission
What, how, who, where, and when…
Never wavering from our future's vision

There's infinitely more fulfillment
In honest and awakened gain
In remaining kind and mindful
And avoiding any future pain…
                              ~Joan Marques

Right livelihood is about the way in which we earn our living. It requires for us to ask ourselves a number of reflective questions: Is my job constructive and not harmful to others? Am I not, directly or indirectly, participating in the production, sales, or promotion of weapons or dangerous tools that can be

© Springer Nature Switzerland AG 2019
J. Marques, *Lead with Heart in Mind*, https://doi.org/10.1007/978-3-030-17028-8_7

used to kill or destroy? Is there any element of slave trade or oppression of others involved in which some people are not paid or heavily underpaid and others take ruthless advantage of that? Am I not contributing to the production of alcohol- and drug-related products that can be dangerous or detrimental to others? Is my job entailing dishonest and unfair practices that prey on others' good intentions and beliefs?

These types of questions can help us to discover whether our work entails wrong livelihood and whether we should consider a change of job or even a change of career. It makes sense that the reflections we engage in to determine right livelihood have a lot to do with other parts of the eightfold path as well. Right livelihood fits right along with right speech and right action, as part of the "moral conduct" section of the eightfold path, which is connected to the earlier mentioned precepts of not killing, not stealing, not misusing sex, not lying, and not abusing intoxicants.[1] Zen Master Thich Nhat Hanh suggests that, in practicing right livelihood, we will have to find a way to earn a living without undermining our ideals of love and compassion. Our daily work should be a worthy expression of your deepest self rather than a source of suffering for ourselves and others.[2]

All that being said, however, it may become clear how difficult it really is to be completely sure that you don't engage in wrong livelihood. You may try to do everything right, but purchase items that come from a person or company that exploits others. You may think that you are selling decent products, but you cannot be completely sure that your suppliers truly acquired or fabricated their products through right livelihood as well. The global business environment of today, in which we deal with stakeholders from many nations and backgrounds, has made this even more complicated than it was before. Sometimes you can also be a supplier of something pure, such as grain, which could be used by one of your customers to brew intoxicating beverages. So, it is complicated, especially if we realize that everything is interconnected, and all we do ultimately leads to the effects we experience around us, the good and the bad ones. This means that, willingly or not, we contribute to good and bad consequences, and our right livelihood can be converted in wrong livelihood by others at any point in the production or service chain.[3]

There could also be instances where a person works for a perfectly sound employer, such as an educational book publisher or a university, where the

---

[1] O'Brien, B. (2018, June 22). *Right Livelihood: The Ethics of Earning a Living*. Retrieved from https://www.thoughtco.com/right-livelihood-the-ethics-of-earning-a-living-450071

[2] Nhat Hanh, T. (1998). *The Heart of the Buddha's Teaching*. Parallax Press, Berkeley, CA.

[3] O'Brien, B. (2018, June 22). *Right Livelihood: The Ethics of Earning a Living*. Retrieved from https://www.thoughtco.com/right-livelihood-the-ethics-of-earning-a-living-450071

main aim is to provide educational materials or practices to customers. Yet, even in those environments, we could run into supervisors that cut corners that want us to practice unethically toward our clients and therefore convert our right livelihood into wrong livelihood. And then there is the issue of working with others, who may push our buttons in the most negative way possible. Is it right livelihood to stay, even if you feel that your spirit suffers every day from a work environment with unpleasant people? A draining job, regardless of how right in absolute terms or how lucrative in financial regards, would still be wrong livelihood for you, because it wears you down. In those cases, it may be wise to consider a change as well.[4]

Right livelihood could also be considered within the broader context of the community in which we live and perform. How are people generally faring in your community? Is there a high level of unemployment, little or no support for the unemployed, weak, and elderly, and poor healthcare for those who cannot afford it? This is also a layer of wrong livelihood, even though you, at the personal level, may be unable to do anything about it. Yet, it is important to have our mind's eyes open and consider these things, because communities that attempt to practice right livelihood will not only work on granting people constructive employment but will also work on ways to help those who are struggling in the most constructive way toward recovery and improved collective well-being.[5]

Finally, we should also be mindful of other effects of our livelihood onto ourselves. If you work so hard and much that your health suffers from it, you are not engaging in right livelihood, regardless of the ethical magnitude of what you are doing. The demands and desires that we pick up from society may influence us to such an extent that we basically abuse our right livelihood in order to make more money, and thus increase our wealth, to an extent that is far beyond what we really need. There is nothing wrong with making money, but if it happens at the expense of your health or the health of those around you, there is something wrong with the picture. At that point, the emphasis of your livelihood has shifted from what you do to what you get, and you should regroup your thoughts. The art is to do the right thing, not only in your practices toward others but also toward yourself.[6] You should make decent money, but you should never push yourself to a degree where money becomes the main focus of your existence, and unfortunately, society

[4] Ibid.

[5] Richmond, L. (2011, March 16). *Buddhism and Wealth: Defining 'Right Livelihood.* Retrieved from https://www.huffingtonpost.com/lewis-richmond/right-livelihood-is-consc_b_832298.html

[6] Sockolov, M. (2016, November 21). Right Livelihood in Buddhism. *Mindfulness.* Retrieved from https://oneminddharma.com/livelihood/

has done a great job in teaching us just that money is critical to purchase almost anything and to get access to things others may not get access to. Yet, money cannot buy us health, well-being, or happiness.

In sum, there are three areas in which you should consider right livelihood: (1) in the type of work you do; (2) in the circumstances at your workplace, and how these affect you; and (3) in the amount of work you do to gain your earnings and how that affects you and those around you.[7]

Let us now consider some extraordinary people who practiced right livelihood.

Millard Fuller's Dream to Provide Others Homes

Life...

Life is a breath
One major respiration
Divided into fragments
of minute exhalation

Life is a breath
Of joy and perspiration
A trial that we share
With varied inspiration

Life is a breath
Of trials and tribulations
A roller coaster ride
With bliss and obligations

Life is a breath
A fly-by-night sensation
That indisputably leads
To our final expiration
          ~Joan Marques

Millard Fuller is best known as the founder of Habitat for Humanity. However, in his early professional years, he was a successful lawyer and entrepreneur, who made millions before he was 30 years old. The downside was that Fuller

---

[7] Ibid.

engaged in wrong livelihood, because he worked almost day and night and oftentimes slept in his office, staying away from his wife and kids regularly in service of the dollars he was earning. So, while they were living in financial abundance, Millard's wife, Linda, was deeply unhappy, and she finally mustered up the courage to tell him that she was planning to leave him. The years of raising their four children all alone while Millard was dedicating all his time to making money had taken their toll. Linda's announcement turned out to be an important turning point in Fuller's life. Millard suddenly realized that his ruthless ambition, solely focused on self-grandiosity and personal wealth, had delivered him a massive bank account but was about to take away the most important people in his life.

After a long and emotional talk, Fuller and his wife decided to give their marriage another chance. In order to do this, they would start from the beginning: they sold their house and other belongings, gave the money to the poor, and embarked upon a search for a new purpose in life. The family moved to a farming community in Georgia, named Koinonia Farm, where they had an old friend, Clarence Jordan, living and working. Jordan's dream was to help those who were in need, and his ideas appealed to the Fullers, so, Millard and his wife became Jordan's partners. They stayed at Koinonia Farm for 5 years while starting simple housing projects with volunteers, aimed at providing a decent quality of life for those in need. In 1973, Fuller and his family moved to Zaire in Africa, now the Democratic Republic of the Congo, to apply their housing model. Three years of successful building in the poorest villages of Zaire convinced Fuller that this housing plan had merit and would work worldwide.[8]

In 1976, the Fuller family returned to the USA, and Millard started a small ministry at Koinonia Farm, gathering a team of volunteers and implementing the housing plan he had further developed in Zaire: building simple but decent houses for low-income community members. The aim of this ambitious project was not personal gain and selfish enrichment this time but progress for the community. Since his wake-up call at 29, Fuller had learned to convert his ruthless ambition, which alienated those around him, to constructive ambition, which attracted increasing crowds of people that wanted to support his cause.

The housing initiative was so successful that Fuller expanded his work into Habitat for Humanity International, in 1976.[9] The way it worked was

---

[8] Alexander, A. (2002). 60 seconds with a CEO: Millard fuller, CEO of habitat for humanity international. *The Greater Baton Rouge Business Report, 20*(18), 19.

[9] Ibid.

that the organization would build homes for the less fortunate ones and only asked back the cost of the materials at 0% interest. The money received was then invested in new building projects. Habitat for Humanity earned respect and commendation from supporters from all walks of life. One of the longtime volunteers of the organization was former president Jimmy Carter, who called Fuller "one of the most extraordinary people I have ever known".[10]

As leader of Habitat for Humanity, Fuller built thousands of homes worldwide, earning him more honors and rewards than he would have ever earned with his old, self-serving mentality. In 1996, President Bill Clinton awarded him the Presidential Medal of Freedom, the US' highest civilian honor. Clinton thereby underscored that Habitat for Humanity was the most successful ongoing community service project in the history of the USA.[11] Millard Fuller has received numerous other forms of international recognition such as the Overcoming Obstacles award from the Community for Education Foundation in New York to Millard Fuller in 2002; the Bronze Medallion from the Points of Light Foundation in Washington, DC, to Millard and Linda Fuller for their pioneering work in service in 2002; Millard's listing as Executive of the Year in 2003 by the "NonProfit Times," and earning the T.B. Maston Christian Ethics Award that same year; and the World Methodist Peace Award from the World Methodist Council to Millard Fuller and Habitat for Humanity International in 2004. Millard has been named Georgian of the year and received a lifetime achievement award from Auburn University, where he earned one of his degrees. In addition to his many awards, Fuller received more than 50 honorary doctorates and authored nine books about his life and his efforts with Habitat for Humanity.

Fuller was a major advocate for expansion of his work. He often explained that there are about 1 billion people in the world that need a decent home, and Habitat for Humanity can only build about 23,000 a year. Therefore, there is place for at least 1000 other nonprofits with a similar focus.

In an interview about his life work, Fuller defined success as the realization and application of the talents one has been given, not for one's own self-interest but for the interest of society as a whole.[12] When asked what advice

---

[10] Millard Fuller, 1935-2009. (2009). Christian Century, 126(5), 17.

[11] Millard Fuller: Habitat for Humanity International Founder. Retrieved on 28 February 2015 from http://www.habitat.org/how/millard.aspx

[12] Alexander, A. (2002). 60 seconds with a CEO: Millard fuller, CEO of habitat for humanity international. *The Greater Baton Rouge Business Report, 20*(18), 19.

he would have for business students, Fuller stated that he would tell them to refrain from using all their resources to themselves but to also consider those around them who have less opportunities or means. He emphasized that humility is a virtue and that all we have been given happened through circumstances beyond our control, including our very life. This understanding, then, may be a guide to consider the mishaps of others and share some of our blessings with them.[13] Another important life lesson Fuller shared was that problems should not be fought but resolved. Fighting problems only leads to more problems, while solving them leads to their elimination.[14]

In spite of his major success, Millard Fuller encountered some troubling times. In the 1990s and later again in 2004, some of the women at Habitat of Humanity complained that Fuller's behavior toward them had been inappropriate. While this was never confirmed, the Board of the organization felt that it was better to release Millard from his duties. In other words, he was ousted from the organization he founded several decades ago. Fuller later commented that the current board of Habitat of Humanity did not have the same ideals as he intended for the organization and that only a few members of this board were spiritually grounded.[15] The board spokesperson, in turn, claimed that times had changed and that the strength of vision and ego, which helped grow Habitat, was no longer the right strategies for the organization today.[16]

The departure from Habitat did not slow Fuller down. He founded the Fuller Center for Housing Inc. and continued his fundraising and building activities until the end of his life.[17] By the time of his passing, the Fuller Center was already active in 25 countries.[18] Millard Fuller passed away after a brief illness in February 2009, at the age of 74, and was laid to rest at Koinonia Farm in Americus, Ga., the place where Habitat and The Fuller Center were founded.[19]

---

[13] Ibid.

[14] Ibid.

[15] Jewell, J. (2005). New times, new leaders: firing of Millard Fuller the result of longstanding tensions. *Christianity Today, 49*(4), 24.

[16] Ibid.

[17] Clements, B. (2005, Oct 07). Controversy hasn't stopped habitat for humanity international founder Millard Fuller. *Daily Record and the Kansas City Daily News-Press.*

[18] Fuller, Millard Dean, 1935–2009. (2009). *International Bulletin of Missionary Research, 33*(2), 75.

[19] Millard Fuller. Retrieved on February 28, 2015 from http://www.fullercenter.org/millardfuller

Andy Moon's Dream to Bring Energy to the Deprived

The Illusion of 'I'

I've come to the conclusion
That 'I' may be an illusion
Because all there is to see
Is not entirely me
This appearance can be changed
These thoughts rearranged
These organs can be replaced
This identity erased
And the spirit or soul…
Is untraceable in the whole
This breath needs air,
which is everywhere.
Once that starts to fade
'I' simply disintegrate
So 'I' am actually a fusion:
a blend, a mass collusion
What's supposed to be 'me':
Is nothing I can see
Therefore, in conclusion,
'I' must be an illusion
                                    –Joan Marques

Andy Moon, still in his twenties at the time this chapter is written, has focused his passion in the area of developing solar energy projects in developing countries. By doing so, he devotes his professional skills to both the environment and international development. Andy is a Stanford University graduate and an alumnus from Y Combinator, an American seed accelerator, which has spawned several successful companies and finds itself consistently ranked at the top of US accelerators.

Andy started his career at McKinsey & Company's Sustainability and Nonprofit practices in New York, where he co-authored widely cited papers on climate change and public health and worked closely with major foundations and multilateral organizations.[20] He would spend his summers in Cambodia and the Philippines, which undoubtedly influenced his awareness

---

[20] Andy Moon (2017). Retrieved from http://www.sunfarmer.org/new-us-team/andy-moon

of the needs in developing nations. His interest in public health grew through his volunteer involvement in the innovative nonprofit "Possible," for which he served as a fundraiser and energy advisor. Possible has a partnership with the government of Nepal to find ways to deliver high-quality, low-cost healthcare to areas in rural Nepal.

In 2009 Andy became a project developer at SunEdison, which focused on building mega-scale power plants in the USA, Canada, and Europe. Through this job, Andy learned the ropes of the solar energy industry. Meanwhile, in 2011, Andy learned from the main physician at Possible that electricity was the greatest challenge for their hospital, because diesel transport for conventional energy generation was costly and sporadic, resulting in just a few hours of electricity being available each day. This severely impeded the efforts to provide high-quality healthcare, and it was obstructing Possible's efforts to expand healthcare services through hospital expansion.[21]

In 2013, Andy started SunFarmer, a nonprofit social enterprise that incubates and launches locally run solar businesses in developing countries. He founded SunFarmer with a co-worker, Jason Gray, and could do this thanks to a grant of $2 million, which he received from a SunEdison foundation.[22] In order to make a solid and responsible start with their venture in Nepal, their inaugural performance ground, Andy and Jason partnered with Avishek Malla, a highly respected Nepali entrepreneur and solar engineer. In this team setting, they installed the first solar energy installation. Once up and running, Avishek joined full-time, and together the three men launched SunFarmer Nepal, a Nepali solar energy company dedicated to installing and maintaining world-class solar installations in Nepal.[23]

In his blog, Andy described a common error that start-ups make and that his company also fell prey to wanting to do too many things at the same time. He explains that, even though he learned at Y Combinator to be cautious about diffusing your focus, his company did just that in its early years, especially because they saw others doing the same thing as well. As was to be expected, however, SunFarmer Nepal soon learned that selling multiple products to multiple customer segments at the same time caused poor performance in all areas. Thanks to some good advice from seasoned solar entrepreneurs, Andy and his team came to realize that their product, solar for farmers, was already very challenging at its core. Any additional focus aside

---

[21] SunFarmer: Our Story. Retrieved from http://www.sunfarmer.org/our-story/

[22] Pipia, A. (2016, March 23). These 24 Americans are changing the world—and they're all under 40 Retrieved from https://www.businessinsider.com/23-americans-who-are-changing-the-world-2016-3# andy-moon-sunfarmer-1

[23] SunFarmer: Our Story. Retrieved from http://www.sunfarmer.org/our-story/

from that would only lead to diminished success. He came across several examples of solar entrepreneurs in other developing nations, who tried the approach of multiple product lines, in hopes to accelerate growth, only to find that there was no growth at all.

Finally taking the lessons to heart, Andy and his SunFarmer's team engaged in a new product development process, identifying a customer segment on which they could focus fully. Their research paid off: they found their target community in the mid-hills region of Nepal where high-value vegetable crops are grown without access to electricity for irrigation in the fields, and with little chance on conventional electricity access, due to the extremely high costs of building an electric grid in such a remote area.

Andy wrote in his blog that his team would only start focusing on another opportunity if this fails, but not until then.[24]

SunFarmer has now installed solar at more than 200 hospitals, schools, businesses, and farms in ten districts of Nepal. Through these energy projects, schools and health clinics were able to receive much-needed power, while disaster victims could be served with appropriate relief. The goal of SunFarmer is to provide power to 4000 hospitals, schools, and water projects around the world by 2020.

In 2017 Andy relinquished the CEO position at SunFarmer, yet he remains actively involved as a board member and advisor. On his LinkedIn page, he describes himself as an entrepreneur that enjoys working on big problems such as energy, healthcare, and politics. He is currently a venture partner at Vas Ventures, focused on supporting early-stage founders.

Wangari Maathai's Dream to Preserve the Environment

Leaf in the Wind

A leaf in the wind
I am,
Floating through time and space.
Purposeless sometimes,
And determined at others.
As if I could change

---

[24] Moon, A. (August 25, 2017). Social Entrepreneurs, Ignore the Mantra of Focus at Your Own Peril. Next Billion (Blog). Retrieved from https://nextbillion.net/social-entrepreneurs-ignore-the-mantra-of-focus-at-your-own-peril/

The destiny of my flight.
Driven by the illusion
That's called ego,
Which takes over
On days that I allow mindlessness
To reign.
But then, I wake up
And regain awareness
Of the breath that I borrowed
To get this body going
Until it's time to pass it on
Like a torch
In the relay race of life,
When the leaf finally lands
In a bed of fertile soil,
In hopes of contributing
To a better tomorrow
For those who will
Continue the flow
After this one.
                              ~Joan Marques

Wangari Maathai is another role model for engaging in right livelihood, even if it meant getting in trouble repeatedly. Born in Nyeri, Kenya, in 1940, Maathai got an opportunity to study in the USA in 1960. She obtained a degree in Biological Sciences from Mount St. Scholastica College in Atchison, Kansas (1964), a Master of Science degree from the University of Pittsburgh (1966), and pursued doctoral studies in Germany and the University of Nairobi, before obtaining a Ph.D. (1971) from the University of Nairobi, where she also taught veterinary anatomy.[25]

She got married, taught at the University of Nairobi, and had three children. However, as the 1970s were approaching their end, so was Wangari's marriage. Her husband could not stand her passionate involvement in political activism, and a bitter divorce followed, in which he accused her of cruelty, madness, and adultery. As her political involvement grew, her educational affiliation waned, and she was eventually evicted from her university home.

In spite of all the turmoil in her life, Wangari was a pioneer in many regards: she was the first female scholar from East and Central Africa to earn a doctorate

---

[25] Wangari Maathai – Biography. Retrieved from https://www.greenbeltmovement.org/wangari-maathai/biography

and the first female professor ever in her home country.[26] Professor Maathai was also the first female to become chair of the Department of Veterinary Anatomy and an associate professor in her field.[27] She played an active part in the struggle for democracy in Kenya and strongly and vocally opposed the oppressive political regime of Daniel arap Moi. In retrospect, Wangari attributed her courage and awareness of the need for a change in Kenya to her five-and-a-half years' experience in America, where she realized that life could be different from what she had known thus far. Her American experience also made her realize that she had a duty to return to her home country and help raise awareness about democracy, freedom of movement, speech, and association.[28] As she was trying to engage in the awareness movement, President Moi and his allies ridiculed Maathai, speaking of her as an overeducated, man-hating dissident. She was pictured as an elitist who was trying to teach innocent African women ways that were not approved by African men. She received numerous death threats, was arrested more than a dozen times, and even beaten unconscious by police at one time. Several of her colleagues were killed, and the Green Belt Movement was nearly outlawed.[29] Yet, it were these bold forms of action that drew attention to the ongoing political oppression—nationally and internationally.

In 1977, Wangari started a grass-roots movement, which would become her life's work. This movement, later known as the Green Belt Movement, aimed at countering the deforestation that was threatening the means of subsistence of the agricultural population. She experienced repeated opposition from the local government but ultimately found support from the Norwegian Forestry Society.[30] The Green Belt Movement was defined as an environmental non-governmental organization focused on the planting of trees, environmental conservation, and women's rights. With her formal education as a powerful ally, Maathai combined science, social commitment, and active politics in her reforestation campaign, which had a powerful effect, as it encouraged women to plant trees in their local environments and to think ecologically. It morphed into a herculean project, and the Green Belt

---

[26] Wangari Maathai – Facts. NobelPrize.org. Nobel Media AB 2018. Retrieved from https://www.nobelprize.org/prizes/peace/2004/maathai/facts/

[27] Wangari Maathai – Biography. Retrieved from https://www.greenbeltmovement.org/wangari-maathai/biography

[28] Gilson, D. (January 5, 2005). "I Will Disappear Into the Forest": An Interview With Wangari Maathai The late Nobel Peace Prize winner talks about sowing the seeds of democracy in Kenya. Retrieved from https://www.motherjones.com/politics/2005/01/root-causes-interview-wangari-maathai/

[29] Ibid.

[30] The Green Belt Movement (2013). "*Wangari Maathai.*" Retrieved from http://www.greenbeltmovement.org/wangari-maathai

Movement spread to other African countries, ultimately contributing to the planting of over 30 million trees.

The funding Maathai received from the Norwegian Forestry Society enabled her to encourage the women of Kenya to create nurseries and plant trees throughout the country and pay for their efforts. Maathai was a brave woman, who got jailed several times during her life, but did not let the threats and setbacks withhold her from fulfilling her mission and exerting what she perceived as right action and right livelihood. Her mobilization of African women was not limited in its vision to work for sustainable development; she actually saw tree planting in a broader perspective which included democracy, women's rights, and international solidarity.[31]

In 2003, as the political climate in Kenya changed and democratic elections had been held, she was appointed Assistant Minister in the Ministry for Environment and Natural Resources, and in 2004 she became the first African woman and the first environmentalist to win the Nobel Peace Prize. The motivation for granting her this highly prominent award was based on "her contribution to sustainable development, democracy and peace".[32] In the formal press release regarding Maathai's nomination for the Nobel Peace Prize, the organization pointed out that peace on earth is related to our ability to secure our living environment. The Nobel Institute felt that Wangari had taken a holistic approach to sustainable development that embraced democracy, human rights, and women's rights in particular. The Green Belt Movement erased the distinctions between environmentalism, feminism, democratization, and human rights advocacy. Maathai was able to see a direct connection between problems such as deforestation and soil erosion and the failures of Kenya's one-party state.[33] In that light, the Nobel Institute also applauded her courage and stated that she inspired many in the fight for democratic rights and especially encouraged women to better their situation.[34]

In 2005, Wangari Maathai was appointed Goodwill Ambassador to the Congo Basin Forest Ecosystem by the 11 Heads of State in the Congo region. The following year, 2006, she founded the Nobel Women's Initiative with her sister laureates Jody Williams, Shirin Ebadi, Rigoberta Menchú Tum, Betty

---

[31] Ibid.

[32] Wangari Maathai – Facts. NobelPrize.org. Nobel Media AB 2018. Retrieved from https://www.nobelprize.org/prizes/peace/2004/maathai/facts/

[33] Gilson, D. (January 5, 2005). "I Will Disappear Into the Forest": An Interview With Wangari Maathai The late Nobel Peace Prize winner talks about sowing the seeds of democracy in Kenya. Retrieved from https://www.motherjones.com/politics/2005/01/root-causes-interview-wangari-maathai/

[34] Wangari Maathai – Facts. NobelPrize.org. Nobel Media AB 2018. Retrieved from https://www.nobelprize.org/prizes/peace/2004/maathai/facts/

Williams, and Mairead Corrigan. In 2007, she lost the local elections in Tetu, barely 3 years after bringing such great recognition to her country by winning the Nobel Peace Prize. Fortunately, Professor Maathai was invited that same year to be the co-chair of the Congo Basin Fund, an initiative by the British and the Norwegian governments to help protect the Congo forests.[35]

Wangari Mathaai died on September 25th 2011 in Nairobi, Kenya, from complications in the treatment of ovarian cancer. Her legacy is still ambiguous, as many younger Kenyans don't even know who she was. While groups of intellectual women, who strive for increased women's rights in Kenya, venerate her for her courage, perseverance, and candidness, others consider her a "bad" woman, because she refused to follow the path of submission and lethargy. In many Kenyan circles, it even seems today that former dictator Moi is more admired than Maathai, simply because Wangari's lifestyle as an educated, divorced, and very vocal woman is not in line with what many Kenyans believe to be the right behavioral patterns for women till today.[36]

The Sacrifices of Right Livelihood

Similar to right view, right intention, right speech, and right action, right livelihood has its share of challenges. Perhaps the challenges of right livelihood are even larger than those of the others, because it is the one element of the eightfold path that pertains to the way we earn our daily bread. We can have great views and intentions and engage in wonderful speech, but when it comes to action, and particularly livelihood, courage is optimally needed.

As we have seen with the three examples in this chapter, each of these individuals went to great lengths to engage in what he or she considered the right thing to do. Millard Fuller gave away all his money and was declared crazy by his friends for allowing himself to be poor again, only to find the right thing to do. Andy Moon, while still young, learned from experience that you have to focus on doing the right thing, and not try to engage in multiple things at the same time. Wangari Maathai was vilified by the government in her country because she wanted democracy and reforestation in a nation where the status quo was submission to corruption and malice.

---

[35] The Green Belt Movement (2013). "*Wangari Maathai.*" Retrieved from http://www.greenbeltmovement.org/wangari-maathai

[36] Nyabola, N. (October 6, 2015). Wangari Maathai was not a good woman. Kenya needs more of them. Retrieved from https://africanarguments.org/2015/10/06/wangari-maathai-was-not-a-good-woman-kenya-needs-many-more-of-them/

If we compare the three leaders discussed in this chapter, we find some interesting commonalities among them: they were all highly educated and extremely smart, all pioneers in the livelihood they chose for the area in which they did so, and all very confident and vocal about what they were doing. They were fearless, even though each of them had to learn some hard lessons and experience setbacks along the way. Yet, in the end, their journey was praiseworthy and set an example for many others to follow.

While Millard Fuller and Wangari Maathai have already passed on, Andy Moon is still very much at the beginning of what will hopefully be a very rewarding career. He has so far demonstrated his value by making a difference in areas where it was considered impossible. Millard and Maathai did the same.

Engaging in right livelihood is not easy, but it rewards infinitely more than continuing to do something that your conscience cannot find fulfillment in.

8

Right Effort

Just Be Good

I have reasons to worry but I don't
In the past I would have – now I won't
The lessons learned in recent years were great
I learned that concern before the time is a useless trait

We worry mostly because we cannot see tomorrow
But in hindsight we realize the futility of our sorrow
All efforts in the world cannot provide any guarantee
For whatever is supposed to be – will be

Our book has been written with conscientious finesse
The outcome is set – whether we stress more or less
While we should not sit around idly and wait passively
We should trust in the goodness of the powers that be

Our best is the best thing we can do
Nice times will come when grim ones are through
Problems get solved in the most unexpected way
Blessings surface on the least predicted day

So, I'm not worried if the future looks a bit bleak
Why should I allow this issue to make me weak?
That future is not here yet
So why should I fret?

© Springer Nature Switzerland AG 2019
J. Marques, *Lead with Heart in Mind*, https://doi.org/10.1007/978-3-030-17028-8_8

Who knows what it's good for?
Who knows where I will be?
Who knows what may be in store?
Who knows what we'll see?

God opens windows
When he closes doors
Just be good
And goodness will be yours…
                    ~Joan Marques

Right effort is sometimes also listed as "right diligence." Effort is a commendable practice, but we can direct it to constructive or destructive activities. People who work in the weapon or drug industry undeniably invest effort in their job, but, unfortunately, this is not right effort, due to the suffering this effort causes.

As is the case with right view (and all other treads of the path), right effort requires that we carefully distinguish our actions, thoughts, and intentions, so that our effort remains constructive.

Right effort is a very personal task, just like all other elements of the path: it also pertains to the act of contemplating about the roots of our suffering and then engaging in the effort to release those roots.

Right effort, along with right mindfulness and right concentration, comprises the mental discipline section of the Noble Eightfold Path.[1] At its very core, right effort entails that we should try to adopt and develop wholesome qualities and behaviors and release unwholesome ones. According to the Pali Canon, the Buddha distinguished four aspects to right effort.

1. The effort to prevent the emergence of unwholesome qualities, such as greed, anger, and ignorance
2. The effort to get rid of unwholesome qualities that you currently have
3. The effort to generate positive qualities that you have yet to acquire, such as generosity, loving-kindness, and wisdom (these are the opposites of greed, anger, and ignorance)
4. The effort to reinforce the wholesome qualities that you already harbor[2]

---

[1] O'Brien, B. (April 15 2018). Right Effort in Buddhism: Part of the Eightfold Path. ThoughtCo. Retrieved from https://www.thoughtco.com/right-effort-450065
[2] Ibid.

It remains important to keep in mind that the elements of the Eightfold Path are not individual steps to be practiced in sequence. They are all interconnected and often happen simultaneously. You can, for instance, only practice right effort, if you practice wisdom, which pertains to right view. Similarly, right effort is translated in your speech (right speech), actions (right action), and the way you earn your income (right livelihood).[3]

Also, right effort doesn't mean "hard" effort, as you should enjoy what you are trying to do. If your effort becomes laborious, you are probably not doing it right, according to the Zen master Thich Nhat Hanh. At the same time, it is still effort, which means that there may be hindrances that can impede you from achieving your goals. A Sutta of the Pali Canon enumerates five aspects that can obstruct right effort. They are (1) sensual desire; (2) ill will; (3) sluggishness, indolence, or lethargy; (4) impatience and anxiety; and (5) ambiguity or skepticism.

Let us now review some individuals who engage in right effort.

Vandana Shiva's Efforts for Fairness in Globalization

On Globalization

What beautiful trend is globalization
If it means progress for every nation
If it entails discarding inequity
And enhancing a balance of quality
But, unfortunately, there's ugly egotism
Fueled and nurtured by ethnocentrism
Where human beings forget their main call
And instead want to rise where others fall
On one hand affluence – inexcusable greed
On the other starvation – devastating need
Rich says to poor: "Open up! Let me in! "
And by doing that, guess who's the only one to win?
Very few wonder how this imbalance started
Very few think back on how wealth once was parted
No need to look back – the future's at stake
Globalization can become anything we make:
An even wider gap through borderless rape

---

[3] Ibid.

Or a beautiful village in honorable shape
A rat's nest of division and infinite hate
Or a unified world before it's too late...
                                          ~Joan Marques

Dr. Vandana Shiva is an environmental activist and one of the leaders of the International Forum on Globalization. She tirelessly campaigns globally against manipulation and monopolization of the global food production by predatory global corporations and advocates biodiversity and indigenous knowledge.

Dr. Vandana Shiva has engaged in this effort since the 1970s and 1980s, voicing the voiceless in regard to environmental sustainability and human wellness, as she perceives it. Shiva takes a critical stance against bio-prospecting efforts undertaken by Western corporations among indigenous communities and advocates social activism to protect communities from exploitation.[4] She has clear viewpoints on the major problems of today's world. She links poverty to the current worldview, which, she feels, allows for a vicious cycle of technologies to compensate for scarcity, environmental destruction, ecosystems disruption, and human poverty.[5]

Vandana Shiva received the first signs of her purpose when she became involved with Chipko, a grassroots movement initiated by predominantly women to enhance awareness about the illegal, massive felling of trees in the Himalayan area, causing vast ecological destruction. Through her involvement in this program, Shiva became aware of the importance of natural resources, the environment and ecology to the poor. Over the past decades, she observed how governments were colluding with big businesses in the depletion of resources and witnessed irresponsible and unsustainable trends in agribusiness and about free trade treaties that supported the monopolization of the global food production through new technologies, making them unavailable to small farmers. The awareness of these mendacious global developments sparked Dr. Shiva's fighting spirit, urging her to found "Navdanya" (meaning "nine seeds") to cultivate seeds and promote biodiversity.[6] Dr. Shiva affirms, "I believe there is a way in which we can move forward

---

[4] Orozco, D., & Poonamallee, L. (2014). The role of ethics in the commercialization of indigenous knowledge. *Journal of Business Ethics, 119*(2), 275–286.
[5] Reason, P. (2014). Justice, sustainability, and participation. *International Journal of Action Research, 10*, 284–309.
[6] Manikutty, S. (2006). An Interview with Vandana Shiva. Vikalpa: *The Journal for Decision Makers, 31*(2), 89–97.

and I try to move in that direction."[7] Being one of the leaders of the International Forum on Globalization, Shiva asserts, "The problem with the current globalization is not because of integration - because we were integrating before and we will be integrating later - but on different terms than the current terms. The current terms of integration are determined by the global corporate layers."[8] She continues:

> What has seriously gone wrong with globalization is the illusion about a global village. The reality is of a global supermarket—run on a Walmart model. Walmart is excellent in maximizing its profit margins, gets cheapest production from wherever it can get, cheapest sales in its retail systems, highest level of monopolizing through economies of scale, and is able to then rip off the workers and the original producers.[9]

Dr. Vandana Shiva continues to lead crusades, partake in forums, and write and speak out about the predatory manipulation of globalization, and specifically, the use of genetically modified crops, which are considered by many to be a major menace to human health and the livelihood of agrarian peoples worldwide.[10] In 2014, she headed a pilgrimage across southern Europe to bring attention to the call from those who want their agriculture to be free of poison and GMOs (genetically modified organisms). Shiva's pilgrimage started in Greece where the international Pan-Hellenic Exchange of Local Seed Varieties Festival was held and then crossing the Adriatic and subsequently travelling by bus through Italy, up to Florence, speaking at the Seed, Food and Earth Democracy Festival. The pilgrims then moved on to the south of France, where they celebrated International Days of the Seed. In all of these activities, Shiva's vocal objections are primarily geared to multinational corporations that generate products of agricultural biotechnology such as Monsanto, a company which she accuses of attempting to impose "food totalitarianism" on the world. In her speeches she repeatedly explains that giant seed companies such as Monsanto are cunningly engaging in the process of engineering, patenting, and transforming seeds into high-priced packets of intellectual property. Shiva claims that they thereby get assistance from major entities

---

[7] Manikutty, S. (2006). An Interview with Vandana Shiva. Vikalpa: *The Journal for Decision Makers*, *31*(2), 92.

[8] Manikutty, S. (2006). An Interview with Vandana Shiva. Vikalpa: *The Journal for Decision Makers*, *31*(2), 94.

[9] Ibid.

[10] Specter, M. (2014). Seeds of Doubt: An activist's controversial crusade against genetically modified crops. *The New Yorker, Annals of Science*, Iss. August 25 2015. Retrieved on March 31 2016 from http://www.newyorker.com/magazine/2014/08/25/seeds-of-doubt

such as the World Bank, the World Trade Organization, the US government, and even philanthropies like the Bill and Melinda Gates Foundation. Through their strategies, Shiva clarifies, these major multinationals are attempting to impose "food totalitarianism" on the world, intending to make all farmers dependent upon their irresponsible and unhealthy products. In her speeches, Shiva portrays two worlds: one with diversity, democracy, freedom, joy, and culture, where people are celebrating their lives, and another filled with mono-cultures and depression. She stresses the importance of small farmers all over the world to maintain their autonomy and their lands, rather than becoming puppets of a global consortium of seed manipulators and earth destroyers.[11]

While Dr. Vandana Shiva is convinced of the rightness of her effort, not everyone agrees with her viewpoints. Those who watch the global population grow at its current pace fear that at the end of the twenty-first century, we may have the volume equivalent of two more Indias in our human population, which will make it impossible for our planet to produce enough food to feed all living beings in a natural way. If humanity keeps growing as it has in past decades, these concerned parties assert the need for GMOs may be the only way to sustain the population. The proponents of GMOs claim that, today, nearly half of the world's soybeans and a third of its corn are products of bio-technology. The GMO proponents claim that genetic modification is as nor-mal a trend in humanity's progress as all other improvements have been thus far. Their stance is that practically all the plants we cultivate, corn, wheat, rice, roses, you name it, have been genetically modified through breeding over time to last longer, look better, taste sweeter, or grow more abundantly.[12]

Yet, Vandana Shiva keeps warning that any seed that is intended for con-sumption and that is bred in a laboratory is unacceptable. To Vandana Shiva, seed is sacred. In Hindi, seed is bija or "containment of life." She says, "Seed is created to renew, to multiply, to be shared, and to spread. Seed is life itself."[13] Nonetheless, Shiva is sometimes opposed even by Indian genetic scientists, who claim that several of her ideas are unfounded or wrongly interpreted. The scientists claim that India could only shift from importing grain to becoming a major exporter of this product in the past decades because of fertilizers and pesticides, which Shiva condemns.[14]

---

[11] Ibid.

[12] Ibid.

[13] *Vandana Shiva and the sacredness of seed* (April, 2009). The Organic and Non-GMO Report. Retrieved from http://www.non-gmoreport.com/articles/apr09/vandana_shiva_the_sacredness_of_seed.php

[14] Specter, M. (2014). Seeds of Doubt: An activist's controversial crusade against genetically modified crops. *The NewYorker, Annals of Science*, Iss. August 25 2015. Retrieved on March 31 2016 from http://www.newyorker.com/magazine/2014/08/25/seeds-of-doubt

Now, genetic engineering is, of course, several steps beyond the use of fertilizers and pesticides. It entails the manipulation of the genes of a seed, so that it counter-attacks its pests due to its own ingrained pesticide. Vandana Shiva fears that the widespread use of GMOs will lead to contamination of all vegetation, even in the wild, thus affecting health of living beings on a massive scale.[15] She passionately keeps stating that fertilizer should never be allowed in agriculture. She considers genetic modification cruelty to seed and abhors the imposed rules of companies such as Monsanto, prohibiting farmers to renew their seed. This is what she refers to as a loss of democracy and a dictatorship on seeds.[16] She has also been known to give another interpretation to GMO, referring to it as God Move Over—we are the creators now.[17]

The war on GMOs has spread thanks to the awareness Vandana Shiva raises globally on agendas of multinationals such as Monsanto. And whether the genetic manipulation of grains is becoming a must in the future or not, Shiva sincerely believes in the rightness of her efforts, along with the fact that in this process, the rich become richer and the poor become poorer.

In regard to the trend of the poor becoming poorer, she has frequently accused the World Bank and the International Monetary Fund (IMF) of manipulating figures to make the global community believe that Indian people have progressed out of poverty massively in past decades. She refutes this by stating that poverty, in her opinion, exists when people cannot provide for themselves, cannot meet their basic needs with dignity, and don't have the freedom of an economic democracy. Shiva opines that since the establishment of the World Trade Organization in 1995, the per capita food consumption of Indians dropped from 177 kilocalories to less than 150, resulting in massive degrees of hunger and malnourishment throughout the country.[18] An Indian-based comparison she made between affluent areas that enjoy subsidies and practice "dumping" reveals how much losses the poorer areas suffer. Dumping, in economic terms, is when a country or company exports a product at a price that is lower in the foreign importing area than the price in their own market.

So, it is within the above-depicted concept that Shiva condemns the way globalization has been implemented thus far, as it is mainly enhancing pros-

---

[15] Ibid.

[16] *Vandana Shiva and the sacredness of seed* (April, 2009). The Organic and Non-GMO Report. Retrieved from http://www.non-gmoreport.com/articles/apr09/vandana_shiva_the_sacradness_of_seed.php

[17] Specter, M. (2014). Seeds of Doubt: An activist's controversial crusade against genetically modified crops. *The New Yorker, Annals of Science*, Iss. August 25 2015. Retrieved on March 31 2016 from http://www.newyorker.com/magazine/2014/08/25/seeds-of-doubt

[18] *Vandana Shiva*. (2014). Canadian Dimension, 48(4), 16–21.

perity for those that were already affluent and keeps depriving the masses in developing nations from any constructive form of growth.

Whether one agrees with Dr. Vandana Shiva's efforts or not, it should be stated that she speaks to the concern of many intellectuals, which is demonstrated by her global following, her many invitations to speak at Universities in the USA and elsewhere, and the many awards she receives globally. In 2003, for instance, *Time* magazine identified Dr. Shiva as an "environmental hero." *Asia Week* has called her one of the five most powerful communicators of Asia. Among her many awards are the Order of the Golden Ark, Global 500 Award of the UN, Earth Day International Award, the Lennon Ono Grant for Peace, and the Sydney Peace Prize 2010.[19] These facts demonstrate that Vandana Shiva has touched many hearts with her efforts and will continue to do so.

Luis Cruz' Efforts to Help the People with Limited Mobility

The Gifts of Today

Whatever gifts you enjoy today
And however many there may be
Use them in a positive way
And share them too – for free

Remember, any gift you share
Is registered by the cosmos
It demonstrates how much you care
It should not be seen as a loss

The gifts you freely grant today
Will be your blessings tomorrow
They'll be repaid somehow – someway
They'll never cause you sorrow

Give love, give peace, give happiness
Give gladly – without resistance
Every gift you grant is your success
Your donation to existence
                                    ~Joan Marques

---

[19] *Vandana Shiva: Biography* (The Right Livelihood Award). Cultivating and conserving diversity is no luxury in our times: it is a survival imperative. Retrieved from https://www.rightlivelihoodaward.org/laureates/vandana-shiva/

When Luis Cruz was 17 years old (in 2010) and a high school student in Honduras, he had a classmate that was a paraplegic. The limited mobility that this fellow student had inspired Cruz, who has a passion for electronics and programming, to invest his efforts in building a device that would help people like his classmate. Luis spend a year to developed the Eyeboard system, which is a low-tech eyeball-tracking device that allows users with motor disabilities to enter text into a computer using eye gestures instead of a physical interface.[20]

The human eye is polarized, with the front part carrying a positive charge and the rear of having a group of negatively charged nerves, which are attached to the retina. When you move your eyes, you can use electrodes to measure the change in the dipole potential of the eye through the skin.[21]

While the Eyeboard system is not a new idea, Luis' brilliance lies in the fact that he made something that usually costs several thousands of dollars afford-able. Cruz' Eyeboard system is built in a set of glasses that cost less than $300.00, which makes it a major breakthrough for humanity, as it means that a technology which normally requires meticulous mapping of direct observa-tions and sophisticated contact lenses has now become accessible to all people with poor motor skills—even those with very little money. Cruz' creation is lo-fi and does not hold the precision of a high-tech tracking system, but it has the ability to track the macro eye movements and can therefore move onto the computer interface software stage.[22]

Luis, a native of La Ceiba, Honduras, a Caribbean port city 252 miles North of Tegucigalpa, sees it as his main objective as a developer and pro-grammer, that is, to use technology as an aid for humankind. His home coun-try, Honduras, is the second poorest country in Central America. Nearly 65% of the population lives in poverty and a lot more people are underemployed. Luis has witnessed quite some health and wellness issues among his classmates growing up.[23] By helping people with disabilities as the developer of the Eyeboard, he believes that he has made a positive change in the lives of many people. Those who have used the Eyeboard say that they have done it primar-ily to help a disabled family member to communicate with other people and

---

[20] *Luis Cruz invented the Eyeboard* (June 21, 2017). Nunnovation. Retrieved from https://www.nunnova-tion.com/2017/06/21/luis-cruz-invented-the-eyeboard/

[21] Blain, L. (November 14, 2011). Teenage Honduran builds open source eye-tracking computer interface for the disabled. Good Thinking. Retrieved from https://newatlas.com/luis-cruz-eyeboard-eye-tracking-computer-interface/20500/

[22] *Luis Cruz invented the Eyeboard* (June 21, 2017). Nunnovation. Retrieved from https://www.nunnova-tion.com/2017/06/21/luis-cruz-invented-the-eyeboard/

[23] Mooney, L. (2016). Luis Fernando Cruz, US Activist for Differently Abled People. *Activists under 30* DOI: https://doi.org/10.1163/9789004377189_004. Retrieved from https://brill.com/abstract/book/edcoll/9789004377189/BP000013.xml

thus improve their way of living. This is how Luis knows that he is successfully contributing toward the advancement of our society. However, as a young philanthropist, he feels that his journey has just begun.[24]

Although the Eyeboard is a fully functioning system, Luis' plan is to keep improving the Eyeboard and make it as affordable as possible. Because he does not have sufficient resources available in his home country, Cruz decided to release the software as open source to speed up development. This means that anyone, worldwide, can access the product's source code and building guide for free. Luis also sells building kits on his website and hopes that interested developers will access the open source code and help improve the Eyeboard.[25]

The Eyeboard is not Luis' only effort to doing things right. He began inventing when he was 14 and can so far already be credited for a number of inventions that have positively contributed to the community, such as the first video game system in Honduras, called the Embedded Entertainment System. Luis was also instrumental in creating the SmartBike, an interactive exercise video game. Each of these inventions has been useful in the advancement of society. This is a great achievement for such a young mind, and Luis feels that his work has just begun. Luis sees entrepreneurship as the foundation of his actions to help improve his community. He considers business a medium to reach out to others, using one's resources to benefit everyone in his or her community.[26]

Fortunately, Luis' efforts have not gone unnoticed. He has been included in Youth Service America's list of the 25 Most Powerful and Influential Young People in the World. He holds a number of awards in various international science fairs, the most notable being his First Place title in the Engineering/ Mathematics Category of the Colorado Springs Science Fair which was hosted by AFCEA.[27]

Luis has a mindset that we increasingly witness among the upcoming generation: rather than considering how he can personally advance from what he does, he wonders how he can help improve society with his innovations. He rightfully feels that this mindset does not only result in an economic plus for one person but can make entire communities fare better. He tries to instill this constructive mindset in other members of his generation as well. His approach is to detect a need and then find out how your skills can help alleviate that need.

---

[24] *Luis Fernando Cruz* (2018). Huffpost. Retrieved from https://www.huffingtonpost.com/author/luis-fernando-cruz

[25] Mooney, L. (2016). Luis Fernando Cruz, US Activist for Differently Abled People. *Activists under 30* DOI: https://doi.org/10.1163/9789004377189_004. Retrieved from https://brill.com/abstract/book/edcoll/9789004377189/BP000013.xml

[26] *Luis Fernando Cruz*. The Extraordinary.org. Retrieved from https://www.thextraordinary.org/luis-fernando-cruz

[27] Ibid.

While he wasn't exactly born in poverty, Luis encountered a lot of poor families in Honduras as he was growing up and realized that there was little advancement in the local community. There was no general sense of collective advancement among members of the society, a culture that was reinforced by the lack of government support. With the encouragement he received from his parents, teachers, and fellow students—he was always very studious and creative—he started testing his entrepreneurial skills by looking around to find out where he could make a positive change. In his process of observing, he learned about what is possibly the biggest problem in third world countries: lack of willpower and support among the community to work together in order to solve local problems. He started exploring technology at 13, and at 16, he built an embedded entertainment system, which ended up becoming the first game system developed in Honduras. He moved to the USA when he got into senior high and met a fellow student who was a paraplegic. This is where the turn of his interest came, and the creation process for the Eyeboard began. As he learned more about the inaccessibility of existing eyeball-tracking projects, he set out to create an affordable version for average people.

Thanks to some assistance he received, Luis could ultimately patent his Eyeboard project and get it to the public. In 2012, the Youth Service America included him on their list of the 25 Most Powerful and Influential Young People in the World.[28]

Maria Mayanja and Her Efforts to Make Non-biodegradable Waste Useful

Just One...

One word
can break or make
a day
Absurd

One smile
can freeze or warm
a soul
in style

---

[28] Ibid.

One shot
can kill or save
a prey
…or not

One heart
can hurt or lift
a man
New start

One universe
can hold or raze
all life
No reverse
   *~*Joan Marques

A promising trend of our times is that more and more young entrepreneurs take on roles that combine economic advancement with social well-being. In Rwanda, a young woman by the name of Maria Mayanja co-founded Angaza Ltd., a company that upcycles non-biodegradable waste into fashion accessories such as bags, wallets, and gadget covers, creating green jobs along the way.[29] As they help restore the environment, these young people also work on the awareness levels of upcoming youth in their country by engaging students in fun, hands-on activities such as tree planting, competitions, and upcycling to engender a more conscious generation of Africans rooted in sustainable practices.

Angaza was founded in 2012 and considers its industry to be in "ethical fashion." With this laudable initiative, Maria expressed her passion for environmental conservation and her drive to help people understand it better in a more simplistic way. On the company's website, Angaza is explained as the Swahili words for "to illuminate" or "to shed light."[30] Through the Angaza project, Maria and her partners aim to take a lead in environmental solutions in Rwanda, hoping to shed light on newer concepts and doing so through innovative creations and community engagement. And of course it's not only about the products but about the entire social advancement that lies behind this initiative: education for youngsters to do the sustainably responsible

---

[29] Conscious Company Magazine (June 1, 2016). 17 Young Social Entrepreneurs Who Are Making the World a Better Place. *EcoWatch*. Retrieved from https://www.ecowatch.com/17-young-social-entrepreneurs-who-are-making-the-world-a-better-place-1891147411.html

[30] Angaza (2018). Our Story: Beautiful is Different. https://angazarwanda.com/story-en

thing, offering green jobs to employable citizens and doing the environment a huge favor by making people more aware of the need to dispose of nondegradable materials. Angaza uses non-biodegradable waste, such as vinyl advertising banners and jute rice bags, and converts them into one-of-a-kind accessories, such as purses, wallets, and various types of bags. The producers line these products with a special fabric, which is called Kitenge in East Africa or Ankarain West Africa. Yet, due to the nature of the products they work with, each item is unique and has no second one like it on the market. This has high appeal to fashionistas.

Maria's entrepreneurial endeavors did not end with Angaza. From June 2015 to November 2016, she was also instrumental in the creation of Impact Hub Kigali, an organization that aims to serve the local community, facilitate collaboration, and drive positive and sustainable change. As was the case with Luis Cruz' projects, it seems that Maria Mayanja's initiative also focuses on encouragement of the local society to step up efforts toward community improvement. Impact Hub Kigali focuses on fostering social innovation. The organization sees itself as a global community, consultancy, and a creative space, working at the intersection of innovation and society to collaboratively create impact with an entrepreneurial mindset.[31]

On Maria Mayanja's LinkedIn page, she states that she ended her employment at Angaza and Impact Hub Kigali in November 2016. At the time of writing this chapter, she served as the student recruitment and marketing officer for Carnegie Mellon University Africa. The current managing director is Monica Umwari.

Challenges and Advantages of Right Effort

An important common quality of the three individuals described in this chapter is that they all represent nations that are still very much struggling to make progress on the global forum. Each of these individuals is also exceptionally intelligent and has the ability to see beyond the obvious. Vandana Shiva, most seasoned and best known in this trio, continues her tireless awareness campaign against multinational corporations, which she perceives as opportunists that take ruthless advantage of the economically weaker ones. Luis Cruz, the young inventor, has also come to an understanding that the journey to making things right is a never ending one. His efforts have always been paid off at least twice, and we are awaiting more news from this young and brilliant

---

[31] Welcome to Impact Hub Kigali. Retrieved from https://kigali.impacthub.net/

mind. Maria Mayanja seems to combine further education with a career in the field at the moment but has already created an immense legacy through the projects that she co-founded, each of which focuses on social awareness and community advancement.

There are thousands of younger and older persons in the world that engage in right effort, who are currently unsung heroes but who incessantly are trying to make a positive difference in their communities. Highlighting the three in this chapter is an indirect way of honoring these unknown heroes as well. Right effort is not always understood or appreciated, especially because human beings perceive matters from different spectrums. Yet, as long as the intentions are right and awareness gets elevated, there is reason to be proud and grateful for these individuals.

As the three stories in this chapter have also demonstrated, right effort cannot be a stand-alone activity: it is closely intertwined with right view, right intention, right speech, right action, right livelihood, right mindfulness, and right concentration.

9

Right Mindfulness

Lost in Existence

Unforgivable is the sense of purposelessness
That awareness sometimes brings
We come – we go
We do what we think we're destined for
But who can tell if it really makes sense?

We struggle – we strive
We try to be the best we can be
We learn, observe, elbow, backstab and engage in politics
Only to find that it did not mean anything
In the whole of existence
Other than a momentary sense of achievement
That got pulverized by the retrospective awakening
And the return to the core of being

Who are we? Why are we? What are we doing here?
We're scraping, building, destroying, reformatting
We discover and invent, and change the status quo
We make progress that leads to regress
And suffer regress that leads to progress
In an unending cycle of living and dying
Uniting, divorcing, laughing and crying
Hopping around with over-inflated ego's

© Springer Nature Switzerland AG 2019
J. Marques, *Lead with Heart in Mind*, https://doi.org/10.1007/978-3-030-17028-8_9

But really not meaning anything in the whole
A purposeless cohort of searching creatures

Lost in existence.

~Joan Marques

When we are mindful, we also engage in right view, right intention, right speech, right action, right livelihood, right effort, and right concentration. In Sanskrit, they use the word "smriti" for mindfulness, and it means, literally, "to remember." Remembering here, means returning to the present moment when we realize that our mind has a tendency to wander. When we are mindful, we see things that we usually take for granted: the grass, the trees, our partner, our colleagues, and our pet, and we realize fully that they are here now. Thanks to our mindfulness, we may be able to truly appreciate what we see, and where there is responding life involved (a person or pet), we may indicate our gratitude for their presence, so that they, too, may become mindful of the moment. The appreciation that is part of such mindfulness can ease the suffering of our usual mindlessness and encourage us to go a step further, so that we concentrate on the other, understand him or her better, and transform our own suffering and theirs into joy.[1]

We can achieve mindfulness in several ways. A frequently practiced way is meditation. One of the most well-known forms of meditation is Vipassana, or insight meditation, which is the meditation practice in which Siddhartha Gautama, generally referred to as "the Buddha," engaged when he became enlightened. Vipassana is now used in various schools of Buddhism to promote attention, awareness, and mindfulness. Vipassana has grown into a global movement and is even more westernized than, for instance, Zen, because it does not require traditional techniques. There are Vipassana meditation centers in all parts of the world. Because it can be practiced in a nonreligious way, it is attractive to Buddhists and non-Buddhists alike.[2]

Vipassana literally means "special seeing" or insight. Since it is a mindfulness technique, Vipassana draws attention to your breath and to every object of consciousness. Business people, academicians, but also prison inmates, seem to experience major transformations when they engage in this meditation practice. For decades popular US sources such as Publishers Weekly and The Philadelphia Inquirer have written about the usefulness of Vipassana for prison inmates, stating that it has helped them break their cycles of anger and revenge. Vipassana is a useful instrument in expanding personal conscious-

[1] Marques, J. (2015). *Business and Buddhism*. Routledge, New York, NY.
[2] Ibid.

ness, and it appeals to people from all religions, cultures, and backgrounds, because it only requires concentration of the mind by observing your natural, normal breathing, without adding any songs, phrases, visualizations, or imaginations.

If interested in doing Vipassana meditation, you will have to start with the obvious: finding a suitable place where you can sit comfortably without interruptions. Wear easy clothes, so that you don't get distracted by tightness or pain. Most people meditate in sitting position. This is particularly useful for beginners. You will develop your most favorite seating position over time. This can be full or half lotus, tailor cross-legged position, one leg in front, kneeling on a soft bench or cushion, or sitting in a chair. Sit straight, yet relaxed, and close your eyes. Focus on your breathing. You can do so by concentrating on the airflow in and out of your nose and sensing how it enters and exits, or you can focus on your abdomen, right above the navel. You will then start experiencing the sense of rising and falling of the breath: as you inhale, it rises; as you exhale, it falls. This is an awe-inspiring activity, which our body does all the time, even when we sleep, yet we pay so little attention to it. Now is the time to focus on the miracle of your breath and release thoughts of past or future. Just focus on your breathing at this very moment.[3]

Your mind may start wandering as you continue breathing. Don't get upset or disheartened. It takes time to take control of this ever-chattering, moving busy body. Once you become aware of the wandering, just bring your mind gently back to the moment, and reconcentrate on your breathing. Don't worry about the nature or contents of your thoughts. Just see them as "thoughts," whether good or bad. Perceive them as an outsider, and redirect your attention back to your breath. To increase your focus, you may think of the movement your breathing makes and speak out the words in your mind: "rising, falling, rising, falling" or "breathing in, breathing out, breathing in, breathing out." While doing so, make sure you don't force your breathing in any particular pattern or speed. Let it happen naturally, as it always does. During your meditation, you will notice the sense of itching, tingling, or tickling. It's something we deal with all the time, but normally don't pay much attention to. During meditation, however, these physical sensations become obvious and may even be experienced as annoying. Don't get upset. Observe your physical sensations with a calm outsider's perspective, and you will find that they will subside. Just like your breathing rises and falls, you will find your physical sensations arising and passing. In fact, observing the arising and passing of your bodily (e.g., itching) and mental (thoughts) sensations is very helpful in realizing that everything in life arises and passes the same way: difficult

---

[3] Ibid.

situations and people but also good ones, they arise and pass. The awareness of arising and passing is critical for understanding the futility of many of the things we frustrate ourselves with.

In the People Business Serving Coffee: Howard Schultz

Peaceful Dwellings

Hazy mountains or lazy rivers
Morning glory or twilight quivers
Wavy oceans with sandy slivers
All are instances of peace givers

Silent nights between the sheets
Quiet parks with wooden seats
Rustling wind through empty streets
Those are also peaceful treats

Yet, these sites, in all their pride
Sooner or later may subside
What better dwelling can peace provide
Than the heart that beats inside?
                                    –Joan Marques

A leader who has displayed mindfulness in multiple facets is Howard Schultz, former CEO of the Starbucks Corporation. As a businessman, Schultz managed to remain mindful of the bigger picture and repeatedly made decisions that were not necessarily in line with a die-hard bottom-line focus.

As a young man, Howard Schultz had majored in Communications at Northern Michigan University. He first worked at Starbucks in 1982, and managed to purchase the company in 1987. His "soft" skills and values helped revive the company at a time when the coffee giant's sales and stock price plummeted. Schultz returned to his role as CEO in 2008 after an eight-year hiatus (he had retired from the CEO position in 2000), and re-ignited the brand through a stubborn mix of passion, love, and inspiration. He had gradually become extremely concerned about the excessive profit focus that threatened to alienate Starbucks from its core activities and remained in the CEO position this time till 2017. Schultz also returned to the CEO position because he felt that growth had become an end onto itself rather than a means to an end. The Starbucks Corporation had turned into a performance machine, where the value of stocks on Wall Street mattered more than the human experience: customers' opinions were no longer important, and neither was the selection of store locations.[4] To Schultz, this development was in stark contrast with his frequently iterated notion of "provid[ing] human connection and personal enrichment in cherished moments, around the world, one cup at a time."[5]

Looking back on the challenge, Schultz explained in the Oprah Winfrey show, "We had lost our way. The pursuit of profit became our reason for being and that's not the reason that Starbucks is in business…We're in the business of exceeding the expectations of our customers."[6] Schultz's first step was to bring together 10,000 Starbucks managers for a 4-day conversation in New Orleans. His purpose? Inspire, engage, and challenge. Within 4 years the company experienced record-high profits, revenue, and stock price.

For Schultz, the secret sauce is not coffee: it's people and relationships. According to Schultz, "Starbucks is the quintessential experience brand and the experience comes to life by our people. The only competitive advantage we have is the relationship we have with our people and the relationship they have built with our customers."[7]

In his book, *Pour Your Heart into It*, Schultz reveals the soul of a storyteller and a deep belief in the dignity of hard work and workers. He manifests himself as a business executive motivated to build an organization founded on values of fairness, respect, and dignity first and great coffee second.[8]

Schultz's gift for inspiring employees stems from his unapologetic humanity and a passion fueled by clear, consistent, and heartfelt values. His ability to connect emotionally with baristas and executives alike is consistently cited as the core of his exceptional leadership skill.

Upon his return as the Starbucks chief in 2008, Schultz closed about 900 underperforming stores[9] and only opened new stores in areas where there was room for responsible growth. Schultz had learned valuable lessons from past

---

[4] Hess, E. D. (2010). Thinking differently about growth. *Financial Executive, 26*(8), 22–25.

[5] Schultz, H. & Jones Yang, D. (1997). *Pour your heart into it: How Starbucks built a company one cup at a time.* New York: Hyperion.

[6] Gallo, C. (2013), What Starbucks CEO Howard Schultz Taught Me About Communication and Success, *Forbes*, 19 Feb.

[7] Ibid.

[8] Schultz, H. & Jones Yang, D. (1997). *Pour your heart into it: How Starbucks built a company one cup at a time.* New York: Hyperion.

[9] Saporito, B. (2012). Starbucks' big mug. *Time, 179*(25), 51–54.

mistakes and used these experiences to the company's advantage from there onward. For instance, when Starbucks was starting to offer breakfast, the aroma of fried eggs was overpowering the well-known Starbucks coffee aroma, alienating many of the coffee-desiring customers. As a result, Schultz became more cautious in introducing new beverages and other products to its line of service. In international performance, Schultz also put his experience to work: no longer did he try to impose Starbucks products to new markets. Instead, he adapted to local desires and cultural directions. Gradually, this led to an increasingly coffee-loving population in tea-admiring nations such as Beijing and Bangkok.[10]

What makes Schultz a particularly good role model for mindful leadership, however, is his sense of responsibility beyond the coffee business. Starbucks' employees, about 160,000 worldwide, are considered "partners" even if they work part-time. Unlike most major employers, Starbucks' part timers receive reasonable pay, full health insurance benefits, and stock awards,[11] a result of Schultz's personal life experience at an early age, when his father was laid off as a part timer without health insurance after an accident. Schultz has also instated college reimbursement programs for employees who work at least 20 hours per week. To that end, he has established partnerships with several US universities. He understands that a college education may lead to a departure of these employees in the long run, but his aim is to contribute to expanded future options for these employees.[12]

Schultz has also been instrumental in assisting with the unemployment problems right after the great recession. Under his guidance, the Starbucks foundation has been supporting a campaign called "Create Jobs for USA," which focused on funding job development in deprived areas.[13] In addition, the Starbucks Corporation has made strides in its listing as a Fair Trade (FT) corporation, thus helping to amplify awareness about this movement, and Schultz has expressed great support for employing differently abled citizens.[14] On his many travels in and outside of the USA, Schultz still talks and listens to many people and engages in initiatives that speak clearly of his will to make a positive difference in other's lives. He has been known to help disabled

---

[10] Lin, E. (2012). Starbucks as the third place: Glimpses into Taiwan's consumer culture and lifestyles. *Journal of International Consumer Marketing, 24*(1/2), 119–128.

[11] Goetz, S. J. & Shrestha, S. S. (2009). Explaining self-employment success and failure: Wal-Mart versus Starbucks, or Schumpeter versus Putnam. *Social Science Quarterly, 90*(1), 22–38.

[12] Choi, C. (2014, Jun 16). Starbucks clears college degree path for workers. *Spartanburg Herald Journal.*

[13] Saporito, B. (2012). Starbucks' big mug. *Time, 179*(25), 51–54.

[14] Marques, J., Camillo, A. A., & Holt, S. (2014). The Starbucks Culture: Responsible, radical innovation in an irresponsible, incremental world. Case study in Palmer, D. E. (Ed.). (2014). *Handbook of Research on Business Ethics and Corporate Responsibilities.* Hershey, PA: IGI Global.

veterans, whom he met on his visits, to find a purpose in life again.[15] He personally assisted in the rebuilding of homes in Louisiana after Hurricane Katrina. Howard Schultz and his wife founded the Schultz Family Foundation, through which many of his social endeavors are sponsored, primarily focusing on rehabilitating veterans in the US economy and assisting young people with low chances in finding work.[16]

The "soft" essence of Starbucks remarkable success is well-described in Howard Behar's 2009 book, *It's Not About the Coffee: Lessons on Putting People First from a Life at Starbucks*. Behar, a 20-year Starbucks senior executive, reveals the ten core leadership principles that drive the company's success. None of them is about coffee. Nor does the list include any "hard" principles associated with traditional command and control management. Rather, Behar touts the virtues of building a culture of mutual trust and defining success by how the company develops its people. Behar attributes Starbucks' success to its genuine commitment to listening, empathy, and "communication with heart."[17]

William Kamkwamba: The Boy Who Harnessed the Wind

That One Dream

Dreams. How long should we cherish them?
And when should we trash them?
I guess no one really knows.
Some people are able to release
The old dream they harbored
As soon as a new one shows
And maybe that's right,
Who am I to judge?
All I can say is
That maybe their old dream didn't mean much…

---

[15] Marques, J. (2017). A Mindful Moral Compass for Twenty-First Century Leadership: The Noble Eightfold Path. *The Journal of Values Based Leadership 10*(1), Article 7.

[16] Anders, G. (March 1, 2016). Howard Schultz's Stormy Crusades: The Starbucks Boss Opens Up. *Forbes*. Retrieved on December 28 2018 from http://www.forbes.com/sites/georgeanders/2016/03/01/howard-schultzs-stormy-crusades-the-starbucks-boss-opens-up/#543c1d45129e

[17] Behar, H., & Goldstein, J. (2009), *It's Not about the Coffee: Lessons on Putting People First from a Life at Starbucks*. New York: Portfolio.

But what if you have one single dream
That you want to realize more than anything
That dazzles your mind
And that makes your soul sing
That tirelessly keeps palpitating
Like a heartbeat: Year after year
Regardless of maturity
Or the fact that old age comes near?

Is that the dream that they call 'the real deal'?
The one that serves the major task
Of keeping you going with a ray of hope
And giving you strength to put up the mask
That you need when you try to endure mediocrity
And celebrate ordinary gobbledygook
While you secretly chase this singular chance
This humongous fish on your emotional hook

I believe that's a dream you should pursue:
The everlasting, hope-giving, reviving one
A dream you should only give up when life is through
When you know all your efforts are finally done.
                                   ~Joan Marques

A young person who used mindfulness to drive his actions is William
Kamkwamba, an innovator, engineer, and author, who was born in Kasungu,
Malawi, in 1987. He grew up in poverty, to the extent that he had to drop out
of school during a famine, which affected the entire village. His family could no
longer afford the $80 annual tuition for school,[18] but William was desperate to
continue his education and discovered the village library as a source for ongoing
self-education. Through his readings he became aware of his love for electronics.
Then, William read a book called *Using Energy*, carefully studied the illustra-
tions in the book, and decided to create a makeshift windmill in 2006 with the
aim of alleviating the needs in his community. He first made a miniature version
with a cheap dynamo, and once he found that it worked, he used blue gum
trees, bicycle parts, and other materials from a scrapyard to create a functioning
windmill that powered several electrical appliances in his family's house. In the
months that he perused the scrapyard across the road from his previous school,
many youngsters made fun of him, and even his mother started questioning his

[18] Wulff, J. (Sept-Oct 2011). The Power of One. Dartmouth Alumni Magazine. Retrieved from https://
dartmouthalumnimagazine.com/articles/power-one

sanity. But William knew what he was doing and incessantly continued his digging and storing of bottle caps, bicycle and tractor parts, and flip-flop rubbers. Once he demonstrated his ability, he had the entire village in awe! He soon wired his entire house, and neighbors would ask if they could charge their cell phones at the home of the Kamkwambas.[19] Generating his own electricity source was a huge accomplishment in a village where only the homes of the very affluent, only 2% of the local population, had their own electricity.[20]

The local newspaper learned about William's accomplishment and wrote an article about it. This got the media ball rolling, and William slowly rose to prominence. A Ted director learned about the young man and invited him to a global Ted event in 2007 in Tanzania. This is when William really became a celebrity. The Ted audience embraced him, and the director went back home with William to see the windmill with his own eyes. He was so impressed by the meticulousness of William's work that he pledged then and there that he would do anything in his power to get this boy to finish high school and get a college education. *The Wall Street Journal* also wrote about his efforts, and William got the long-desired opportunity to go to college. Many media outlets interviewed him and he served as a guest speaker at several global events. Engineering professors referred him as "natural" since he had been able to build such a complicated device with no tools other than a few nails.

The news spread like wildfire as William continued his efforts: he built a solar-powered water pump to supply drinking water in his village and two other windmills. In 2013 *Time* magazine named William one of the 30 People Under 30 Changing The World. Meanwhile, in 2009, William had written a book about his story, titled, *The Boy Who Harnessed the Wind*.[21] With the book being selected by public library systems to cover entire communities, and being donated to many youngsters through gift funds, William soon had a bestseller on his hand! *The Boy Who Harnessed the Wind* managed to remain on *The New York Times* bestseller list for a full 5 weeks![22] In 2014, William Kamkwamba graduated from Dartmouth College in Hanover, New Hampshire.

Thanks to his great effort, his mindful practice, but definitely also his awe-inspiring and pleasant mannerisms, Kamkwamba now has a whole team of experts to turn to. Yet, his fame has not changed his sober outlook on life. While life in abundant societies has been pleasant, he has not forgotten where he came from and that he and his family once lived on four spoons of por-

---

[19] Ibid.
[20] Ibid.
[21] Ibid.
[22] Ibid.

ridge a day to survive a terrible famine. He has created a nonprofit called "Moving Windmills," which now sponsors the local soccer team in a deliberate effort to keep youngsters from drug use and loitering. He helps put his sisters through school by paying their tuition out of his own pocket. He continues to work in his village and continues to examine areas of need that he can alleviate with his skills. He has built a deepwater well with a solar-powered pump that his entire village can access. Thanks to this project, women in the village are now spared a 2 hour walk to a public well. William also just opened a maize-grinding mill, which will guarantee a steady income for his family. He is also rebuilding the local primary school, to give all children in the village a chance to get an education. In addition, he has started an evening adult literacy program to also bring education to older members of the community.[23]

Gisela Solymos: Finding Inclusive Ways to End Malnourishment

Contamination

As the dirty water seeps
From the outdoor 'room of ease,'
Forming a fusty puddle, in collaboration
With dry leaves, rotting olives,
And multiple legions of bacteria;
Unwary children, varying from one to eight,
Plant their bare little feet in the soaking clutter
And enjoy the sensation of sludge between their toes
Unaware of the danger they are exposed to
Or the upcoming hysteria
Of mothers who will, once again, witness
The contagion of yet another little one
Slowly slipping out of their feeble hands
In a detrimental environment:
The quintessence of archaic deliria
While, in other parts of the same world,
Shoes, clothes, indoor sanitation and food
Are among the normalcies of daily life
And not – as in their universe -
Part of an unattainable set of criteria.

-Joan Marques

---

[23] Ibid.

When she was merely 5 years old, Gisela Solymos saw an undernourished homeless man. She was so taken by the sight that she started thinking from then on how she would be able to solve the problem of malnourishment.[24] Gisela, daughter of a Hungarian father and Brazilian mother, learned from her dad to become a high achiever. She inherited his natural curiosity and brightness and grew into a curious youth, who harbored a high level of sensitivity and compassion for others. In her teenage years, she joined a group of youngsters who worked in a favela, a Brazilian slum. This experience had a profound effect on her and shaped her focus on a future professional direction even more: she wanted to do something to address the deplorable circumstances she saw.[25]

She was an intelligent lady and focused her education on psychology, earning her bachelor's degree in 1987. She started her career as a clinical psychologist working with children with learning disabilities, while she also started exploring options to get her project for better nutrition of the poor and downtrodden funded.[26] She opened a private clinic to treat children with learning disabilities but was forced, through the local financial crisis, to close her office and look for other work. Life led her even deeper into her calling, when she became a field researcher surveying the socioeconomic and nutritional conditions of residents of the Vila Mariana Favela.[27] Along with her team, Gisela started working on a structure for health intervention in this community. She did so by paying house visits and investigating what the healthcare and support needs were among these poor families.[28]

In 1993, Gisela Maria Bernardes Solymos became the co-founder of CREN, the Center for Nutritional Recovery and Education, a Brazilian non-profit entity that focuses on preventing and treating child malnutrition. Malnutrition is a critical element of extreme poverty. In the Brazilian city of São Paulo alone, there are about 1.7 million people that live in slums, where families have very low schooling and are either underemployed or unemployed. The unhealthy living conditions spread to family health issues, augmented by unhealthy housing conditions that expose children to recurrent infections. Most people in these slums are uninformed; entire families live an

---

[24] Gisela Maria Bernardes Solymos (2013). Visionaris. Retrieved from http://ubs-visionaris.com.br/finalistas-2013/179-gisela-maria-bernardes-solymos

[25] Gisela Solymos (2018). Ashoka Fondation. Retrieved from https://www.ashoka.org/en-US/fellow/gisela-solymos#intro

[26] Gisela Maria Bernardes Solymos (2013). Visionaris. Retrieved from http://ubs-visionaris.com.br/finalistas-2013/179-gisela-maria-bernardes-solymos

[27] Gisela Solymos (2018). Ashoka Fondation. Retrieved from https://www.ashoka.org/en-US/fellow/gisela-solymos#intro

[28] Ibid.

isolated life, with several members abusing drugs and other substances. Family violence and sexual abuse are also part of the unwholesome circumstances in these slums. Given the abundance of struggles living in these slums brings, it is not strange that malnutrition, in the form of undernourishment or obesity, is a recurring problem. In the case of obesity, the problem is that people substitute dissatisfactory and unaffectionate relationships for food. So, malnourishment, in either way, is a family psychological issue.[29] Gisela, thanks to her educational background in psychology, realized that and was instrumental in creating a multidisciplinary, all-encompassing approach at CREN, entailing professional training programs, nutritional education, prevention and fight against child malnutrition, courses for the Family Health Program teams, partnership with universities, and technical assistance to national and international programs in the areas of health and nutrition.[30]

In fact, Gisela has worked tirelessly on making CREN stand out from its very beginnings and accomplish its goals in the most constructive ways possible. The difference Gisela and her team members established between CREN and other organizations that work with malnourished children is that CREN involves the entire family in the process toward healing and therefore does not separate the child from his family. In addition, CREN tries to address the root of the problem through education, as described above. In that regard, the organization works with schools to educate communities on nutrition. CREN's activities have currently benefited over 50,000 children throughout Brazil.[31] When considered on a broader scale and including the families affected by the work of this organization, CREN has benefited almost 3.5 million people in Brazil, Latin America, and Africa.

In recent years, Gisela devoted much of her efforts on completing the restructuring of the organization's governance. To that end, she became a member of CREN's managing board. Having ensured that CREN is managed well, Gisela engaged in a partnership with Icensa (University of Notre Dame) and GAF, in order to spearhead a new initiative aimed at integrating different types of knowledge and technology to have a more accurate vision of the root causes of child malnutrition and obesity and of successful and scalable solutions. As a psychologist, Gisela has a unique view of malnutrition and has been studying the immense suffering that is associated with it with the aim to help the patients as well as their loved ones. She also went ahead and earned a

---

[29] Gisela Solymos (2018). Ashoka Fondation. Retrieved from https://www.ashoka.org/en-US/fellow/gisela-solymos#intro

[30] Ibid.

[31] Schwab, H. (April 18, 2012). The Latin America Social Entrepreneurs of the Year. Retrieved from https://www.huffingtonpost.com/hilde-schwab/latin-america-social-entrepreneurs_b_1435423.html

Masters in Psychology and Human Development (USP, Brazil), as well as a PhD in Social Psychiatry (UNIFESP, Brazil). She is also a Schwab Foundation Social Entrepreneur, an Ashoka Fellow, and a member of the NCDs Dialogue Series Steering Committee of the World Economic Forum.[32]

Gisela is still a vibrant and creative spirit, perceiving CREN as an ever-evolving entity, with continuous attunement into the needs of children in poverty and the challenges their environments bring.[33]

The Golden Path of Right Mindfulness

When you practice right mindfulness, you make sure that the steps you take toward anything you plan to do are well-considered and responsible. Most of the time, right mindfulness leads to positive long-term outcomes, because mindfulness is a practice that considers more than just this very moment. The three individuals discussed in this chapter are mere examples of how mindful behavior can determine the course of a life.

In the case of Howard Schultz, he had faced hardship and disappointments as a young man but also learned that he had to do right with those he would work with in the future, based on the misfortune he witnessed in his father's career. In order to do right, he had to be mindful in the steps he would make toward that future. When he visited Europe and saw the model that would later become Starbucks, he knew there was a major chance that this would work in the USA but also understood that he would need help from others to start and to make this project work. The key was in treating people right from the very start. Starbucks built a reputation in the past decades for its treatment of stakeholders. This is mindfulness in action in the case of a for-profit business.

In the case of William Kamkwamba, mindfulness flourished at a very early age as well and was also induced by hardship. Enduring a terrible famine, seeing many people suffer and die, and finding out that education was a privilege that was no longer within reach, made William determined about reaching his goal and making sure that he would benefit as many people as possible along the way. When he worked on the windmill project, he was well-aware that this would bring development in his village, and for each project afterward, the bigger picture remained part of William's mindful performance.

---

[32] Schwab Foundation for Social Entrepreneurship in partnership with the World Economic Forum (2018). Awardees: Gisela Maria Bernardes Solymos. Retrieved from https://www.schwabfound.org/awardees/gisela-maria-bernardes-solymos
[33] Ibid.

In the case of Gisela Solymos, it was also the confrontation with hardship and the massive suffering of large groups of people that propelled her to study psychology and urged her to focus on treating malnourishment in a comprehensive fashion. Gisela understood that problems of this magnitude cannot be solved by just addressing the problem at an individual level. This had to be approached systematically, through awareness enhancement from all parties involved. Gisela made mindful choices in life and is still on a path to engage in mindful practices that continue to benefit those in need.

As the stories in this chapter also demonstrated, right mindfulness is not a stand-alone practice. It requires right view, in order to see the reason for the path to move onto. It requires right intention to look in the right places for support and engage in the right practices toward succeeding. It requires right speech to convince different people and institutions why your views and intentions are worth their while. It requires right action, because you cannot get anything done without a well-balanced and deeply considered action plan. It requires right livelihood, because your mindful practice will not allow you to do something that is unacceptable for your value system. It requires right effort to invest time, insights, knowledge, persuasion, and so much more in making the project happen. It also requires right concentration to stay focused throughout the distractions that life will bring.

10

Right Concentration

Lost in Details

…is where we are
from day to day
when we struggle and strive
and get confronted with challenges
that are minuscule in the whole
of existence,
but that become our entire focus
of the moment…
when we try to prove ourselves
be popular, beautiful, wanted, needed…
when we chase opportunities
that are as fickle as air
because they will be gone
the next instant…
Lost in details
while the whole
passes us by

　　　　　　　　　　　　~Joan Marques

Right concentration has everything to do with focusing on what is important. Sometimes it is important to focus on one particular thing, such as our breathing when we engage in Vipassana meditation (explained in previous chapter). At other times it is important to concentrate more actively on a set of activities. An example is driving: when we drive, we focus on our driving, but also

© Springer Nature Switzerland AG 2019
J. Marques, *Lead with Heart in Mind*, https://doi.org/10.1007/978-3-030-17028-8_10

on the lights, other vehicles on the road, people crossing the streets, our speed, the condition of the road, the direction in which we are going, possibly on the rain, and so on.

We have to concentrate in order to be mentally present, and when we do that, we experience each moment to the fullest. When we focus fully on each moment instead of constantly thinking about the past and the future, we may discover beautiful details in the here and now that would have escaped us if we were not concentrating. Right concentration can therefore offer us greater happiness in the current moment, as we are more focused on what matters now. Also, right concentration can help us realize more than anything else, that everything is temporary. Our feelings of aggravation or anger and our feelings of euphoria: they eventually subside. Thanks to our concentration, we can thus learn to see them in their right scope: as fleeting senses, which we can release if we want to.[1]

Right concentration is interrelated with the other elements of the Noble Eightfold Path.

Right concentration is sometimes also referred to as right meditation. Right mindfulness and concentration are both tools to sharpen the mind.[2]

Identifying a leader to model right concentration is not impossible, but is slightly more complicated, due to the specific focus in concentration. At the same time, it's important to emphasize again that the individuals presented in this book so far could be placed interchangeably, because each element of the Noble Eightfold Path is interwoven into the others.

Abdel Alzorgan's Dream for a Motivated Youth

A New You

There'll never be another you
Not even after the next blink
This moment is your only one
It's more precious than you may think.

Even as you read this you change
Through awareness and natural maturing

---

[1] Thich, N. H. (1998). *The heart of the Buddha's teaching: Transforming suffering into peace, joy, and liberation.* New York: Broadway Books.

[2] Nouri, D. (May 3, 2013). What is the Eightfold Path? *Secular Buddhist Association.* Retrieved from http://secularbuddhism.org/2013/05/03/what-is-the-eightfold-path/

Your cells, thoughts, insights, skills
Always evolve – they're not enduring

The person who acted in the past
Has long transformed – and didn't last
The one who will act tomorrow
Will be shaped by future joy and sorrow

But you're here now – where you should be
It's vital, even if you cannot yet see
It's the foundation of a new "you"
To be born when this moment is through
                                    ~Joan Marques

Born in 1990, Abdel Alzorgan worked with his father, a local former in Talifa, Jordan, from a young age on. His father was a kind and encouraging dad, who was well-respected in the local community due to his helpful attitude. However, the family had little money and lived a modest, frugal life. He soon learned about a structural problem that all local farmers were struggling with: not enough water and no frost protection for their crop during winter. This caused a large part of the harvest to dry up, mold, or rot every year. So, along with his brother Mohammad, Abdel started studying ways to develop a system that would ensure more responsible and sustainable water usage and safeguarding the crop during winter.[3]

The brothers made good progress with their science project, but encountered a problem: they needed money to take their research to the next level, where they could buy the necessary equipment and test the system. So, the boys started looking for ways in which they could find sponsorship. They learned about a local science fair and entered their project. They won, and this was the first step in getting their name out and earning some recognition within the local community. As a next step, Abdel and Mohammad entered their project in a larger forum, the INTEL International Science and Engineering Fair. They did this in 2006 and in 2008, and in the last submission, they won fourth place, which gave the boys an opportunity to travel to the USA.[4] This visit to the USA was a life-changing experience for Abdel and his brother. First of all, they had to learn English, which they did by watching

---

[3] Horsfield, P. (2018). Abdel Rahman Alzorgan. *The Extraordinary.org*. Retrieved from https://www.thextraordinary.org/abdel-rahman-alzorgan

[4] Hannah, J. (2018). Incredible Humans: Abdel Alzorgan is a dreamer we can all get behind. *Six Two*. Retrieved from https://sixtwo.ctk.io/six-two/abdel-alzorgan/

a lot of English programs on television. They also had to practice their presentation extremely well. Interestingly, Abdel found that if you want to realize your dream you have to sleep less.[5]

Throughout these opportunities, Abdel and Mohammad developed a unique sprinkler and water conservation system that did not only irrigate the crops but also protected them from frost during the winter. This new system from Abdel and Mohammad was not only beneficial for their family: all the local farmers could use it and benefit from it. The sprinkler initiative planted a seed of passion within Abdel, and he wanted to accomplish more for his community, and especially his peers. He had found out, by then, that many of his local peers were not as passionate as he was to accomplish great things for their community. Abdel realized that the inspiration he received from his father was critical to the way he perceived education but that it was not necessarily the way every youngster saw it. Where he thought that the desire to obtain an education would be every youngster's dream, he discovered that this was not the case. He knew he had to do something in order to change the tide, and what would be better than to become a role model?[6]

Upon getting the opportunity to visit the USA as the fourth place recipients of the Intel International Science and Engineering Fair, Abdel learned a few important differences between this country and his own: first of all, young people had instant access to information and could get all the training they desired in a very easy manner. This was much harder for the youth in Jordan. He realized that this visit may have been a sign for him to tread a path that no youngster had treaded before: becoming an inspiration to his fellow young Jordanian citizens.[7] Upon his return to Jordan, Abdel started realizing his vision. He accepted opportunities to speak before audiences of young people and inspire them with his story and his insights. All the while, he also understood that he had to walk his talk, so he made sure he finished secondary school, followed by Talifa Technical University, where he studied Mechatronics Engineering, and that his grades were stellar. Then he got an invitation to speak at a TEDx event. He saw this as a huge privilege and a great opportunity to reach an even larger audience and empower even more youngsters to understand that they had the power of a better future in their hands.[8]

---

[5] Horsfield, P. (2018). Abdel Rahman Alzorgan. *The Extraordinary.org*. Retrieved from https://www.thextraordinary.org/abdel-rahman-alzorgan

[6] Abdel Alzorgan (2019). *Oath Inc. – Huffpost News*. Retrieved from https://www.huffingtonpost.com/author/abdel-alzorgan

[7] Ibid.

[8] Horsfield, P. (2018). Abdel Rahman Alzorgan. *The Extraordinary.org*. Retrieved from https://www.thextraordinary.org/abdel-rahman-alzorgan

One thing led to another, and Abdel, now a well-known young role model in Jordan, was named ambassador for One Young World, an organization focusing on the empowerment and education of youths around the world. One Young World brings together the greatest youth minds in the world and creates pathways for them to optimally utilize their potential and become exemplary members of their societies. Now invited to forums beyond his home country, Abdel was soon identified as one of the 25 Most Powerful and Influential Young People in the World in 2012. The eye of the international community was now fully on Abdel and his great empowering work for youngsters.

The success story described above should not be seen as an uninterrupted chain of windfalls. Abdel had—and still has—his setbacks as well. Yet, while he can get down from them, he makes sure he doesn't stay down. He always gets up, evaluates his mishap, wonders how he can learn from it, and uses it to encourage others as well. He also makes sure to always explain the deeper purpose of obtaining education to the young people he reaches. Thanks to Abdel's right concentration, he realizes that there is a major difference between breathing and being alive. So many people just exist, because they are not motivated, and this robs them from the opportunity to really enjoy a rewarding life. Lack of motivation is a peril to the quality of anyone's life. On the other hand, inspiration is the most important way to change a person's life for the better, and with that, help change the future for themselves and their community. Abdel, who is now labeled an inventor, a water conservationist, and an activist, has a mantra, which is that inspiring the youth equals changing the world. He strongly believes in the power of dreams and encourages his audiences to dare dreaming toward a better future.[9]

Kendall Ciesemier's Compassion for Kids

Despair

Sometimes I can't breathe
Because of all the suffering
I am aware of in the world
Kids starving from hunger
And animals abused
By ignorant people
Who lost their sanity

---

[9] Ibid.

Or their sense of humanity

Sometimes I have a hard time
Seeing the purpose of my work
Because, while I contribute
There are so many needs
That I cannot fulfill
Needs, more direct and dire
That require a moral code
In a massively collective mode

Sometimes everything seems hopeless
Because it's the way of the world
At the core, a chaotic mess
Of self-centered entities:
People, cities, nations…
Identifying with a few
And simply disregarding the rest
Oh, what an abominable pest…
                                    ~Joan Marques

When Kendall Ciesemier was only 11 years old, she watched an Oprah Winfrey show that highlighted AIDS orphans in Africa. Having had her share of health struggles in life, Kendall could vividly envision the despair that so many of these orphans were going through, having to take care of their younger siblings, yet with no security for their own future. At the same time, she was awestruck by the dogged hope these young children, many of her age or younger, displayed in their struggle for life. This became a decisive moment in Ciesemier's life.[10]

Born in Wheaton, Illinois, in 1993, Kendall struggled with a rare liver disease called biliary atresia, a defect where the bile duct—which is supposed to be present between the liver and the small intestine—is either blocked or is absent. In Kendall's case, her bile duct was blocked, which meant that she had to be extremely cautious with anything she took in.[11] Kendall had loving parents, who had the means to support her sufficiently and who made a lot of sacrifices to comfort their daughter, a fact, which she gratefully recalls today.

---

[10] Ciesemier, K. (2013). My Name is Kendall: This is My Story… *MyNameMyStory*. Retrieved from http://mynamemystory.org/kendall-ciesemier.html
[11] Horsfield, P. (2018). Kendall Ciesemier. *The Extraordinary.org*. Retrieved from https://www.thextraordinary.org/kendall-ciesemier

Ultimately, however, the health problem caused Kendall to undergo two liver transplants at a time when other youngsters were only concerned or excited about their next technological gimmick or their next social media posting. She got the first half of her liver from her father, and the other from a donor, but had to remain hospitalized all summer to ensure that her body would not reject the new liver.[12]

Having seen the program about the AIDS orphans in Africa drew Kendall to start searching for other children in the world who were struggling, yet did not have the means to make any progress. Her first gift was a $360 donation to a then 8-year-old girl from Mauritania without parents, named Benite, who could finally dare to dream of a future by enrolling in school, thanks to Kendall's support. Establishing this connection with another youngster who also experienced major challenges in life gave Kendall a strong sense of purpose, and she decided that her path would be to do whatever she could to help other kids in need. She made "Service is my Power" her mantra and started raising money, from family, friends, but also other children who learned about Kendall's efforts and wanted to help. In the summer of 2004, Kendall had raised, with the help of all these known and unknown "angel investors," the sum of $15,000 and could she sponsor an entire village in Zambia, named Musele.[13]

In 2005, when Kendall was barely 12 years old, she received assistance in converting her project Kids Caring 4 Kids (KC4K) into a 501(c)3 not-for-profit organization. Her purpose with this organization was to inspire kids in the USA to care for and support those in need. Kendall's main focus was to awaken empathy within kids, living under more fortunate circumstances, for those who experienced far greater challenges and fewer opportunities, such as the AIDS orphans in Africa. Kendall was compelled to bring better living circumstances to these kids, including education, food, clean water, shelter, transportation, and hygiene.[14]

In order to spread the word, Kendall took to schools, youth groups, and service organizations and invited them to get involved. Fortunately, many of them did just that, and several organized tournaments and other events as fundraising activities to support the cause of KC4K. It is amazing what a concerted and devoted effort with a right mindset and concentration can accomplish. Since she started her not-for-profit, Kendall has been able to

---

[12] Ibid.

[13] Ciesemier, K. (2013). My Name is Kendall: This is My Story… *MyNameMyStory*. Retrieved from http://mynamemystory.org/kendall-ciesemier.html

[14] Ibid.

sponsor eight projects in four African countries. Among those projects are building a dormitory and 2 orphan centers and providing 400 specially built bikes, school supplies, medical care, indoor plumbing, healthy meals, and boreholes to increase the quality of life for these African kids. Her dedicated work caught the attention of major celebrities in the US society, such as Oprah Winfrey and President Clinton. Kendall is particularly proud of the fact that her work represents a concerted effort of children to help other children. It all started with stepping away from the image of Kendall, the sick girl, to Kendall, the girl who helps other kids, but it mushroomed into something much broader than that. Kendall keeps inspiring youngsters till today to continue giving by way of finding a purpose, since it is so rewarding to help a person in need. Kendall Ciesemier has received multiple awards for her philanthropic work. Prudential and the National Association of Secondary School Principals have named her one of America's top ten youth volunteers. She has also been listed as 1 of the 20 Amazing Young Women of Glamour magazine and won the Woman of the Year Reader's Choice Award.[15]

Kendall made sure that she also remained an inspiration to young people, by doing very well in school and, afterward, accomplishing some important career advancements aside from her volunteerism. Having learned about the power of media at a very young age, she has emerged into a talented journalist, serving as correspondent for several major news sources such as The Daily Beast and Newsweek.[16] She cleverly uses media for both her passions: her journalism career and her volunteering projects.

What makes Kendall such a respected and appreciated young woman is the fact that she has not been unscathed by life's twists. As a child she got confronted with the fact that she might not make it too long, given her liver disease, and this helped her face the impermanence of things from a very young age on and made her realize that the best way to demonstrate gratitude for the chance she received on life was to help other children get that chance as well. Her youth illness made her fearless in her pursuit to do the things she was most passionate about in life, and today, she feels compelled to share this passionate message with others as well.

Today, Kendall Ciesemier is described as an activist, a journalist, a writer, and a social entrepreneur.[17] She has successfully completed her education at

[15] Horsfield, P. (2018). Kendall Ciesemier. *The Extraordinary.org*. Retrieved from https://www.thextraordinary.org/kendall-ciesemier

[16] Ibid.

[17] Harrison, C. (Nov 7, 2018). New York Film Academy (NYFA) Documentary Alum Kendall Ciesemier Talks Activism, Social Causes. *New York Film Academy*. Retrieved from https://www.nyfa.edu/film-school-blog/nyfa-alum-kendall-ciesemier-talks-activism/

Georgetown University, has managed to juggle her hectic study schedule with managing KC4K, and meanwhile also co-founded OWN IT, a women's leadership initiative to empower college-aged women to engage with women leaders.[18] At the time of writing this chapter, Kendall was a producer at digital news company Mic, where her focus ranges from criminal justice reform, racial justice, the #MeToo movement, and more.[19]

The Reward of Right Concentration

Be Happy Here and Now

Be happy here and now
For tomorrow, the standards may have changed
And the factors that are in place today
To contribute to your happiness
May have altered
And the perceptions that you currently sanctify
May have shifted
And the living ones you surround yourself with
May have expired or transformed
And the environment, the values, or the circumstances
May have metamorphosed
Into a shape, direction, or magnitude
That you had not foreseen
And that will direct you toward new definitions
Of what happiness is… then.
~Joan Marques

---

[18] Ibid.
[19] Ibid.

11

Living and Leading with the Eightfold Path

Touching the Wind

My spirit touched the wind today
As I enjoyed the delight of my sight
A trio of merry leaves swirled down
And laid by my feet ever so light

A sleepy woman slowly walked by
Pillow lines still visible in her face
That desolate tune emerged again
The one my heart tried to place

How can one catch a naked melody
With no words around it wrapped?
Oh mental maze – oh endless trial
Keeping this poor psyche trapped!

A huge gray cat peered into the world
As my mind's eye inspected my soul
This beautiful, fickle moment in time:
Would it mean anything in the whole?

How many more rounds for me to go
On this seemingly eternal carrousel?
Familiar names and faces –to and fro
To a destination no one could tell

© Springer Nature Switzerland AG 2019
J. Marques, *Lead with Heart in Mind*, https://doi.org/10.1007/978-3-030-17028-8_11

And suddenly there was a glimpse
Of silent sadness without console
A smile, lost forever, faintly emerged
Before my autopilot regained control

My spirit touched the wind today
And made an emotional dive
It remembered all that came and went
In this, my current life
                                   ~Joan Marques

Leadership Is a Personal Choice

Leadership is, ultimately, a very personal thing. You can read as many theories and hear as many stories as you want, but in the end, you will make the decision in regard to the path you will tread, the way you will treat others, and how you will carry yourself through different circumstances.

Keeping the Noble Eightfold Path in mind is always a good idea. And, as stated throughout this book, the eight treads of this path are interrelated. Right intentions emerge from right views and incite right efforts and right actions. A point of caution is in place here: just as the right interpretation of all elements of the path are interrelated and supportive of one another, just so are malicious implementations and interpretations interrelated and mutually supportive. In other words, you can get trapped by wrong intentions, wrong views, wrong efforts, wrong actions, and so on and maybe even believe they are right, because the human psyche is a miraculous thing: we stand on different sides of reality, and what some of us may consider right, others may consider dead wrong.

Because it is all so personal, your only true guide will be… you! Try to engage in insight meditation, even if it initially seems hard to do. We are living in dazzling times, where even five quiet minutes seem like forever, so engaging in 20 or 30 minutes of meditation may seem like an impossible chore. But practice makes perfect, and if you allow yourself to follow your breathing and decide not to get upset if you catch your mind wandering, you may ultimately get the hang of it—all by yourself.

The broad cluster of individuals you were exposed to in this book were deliberately "recruited" from multiple environments and multiple parts of the world. Many of them were still young at the time of writing this book, and perhaps that explains what some may consider "their idealistic view of the world." Yet, there is no denying that they found satisfaction, recognition, and much appreciation through what they were doing. And, human beings that they are, they got encouraged by the feedback they received from their communities.

The deeper intention with exposing you to all these people is to identify. Hopefully, one or more of the presented "leaders" reminded you of something you did, believed in, or aspired. You don't have to become famous to be a good leader of your life.

Let's first briefly summarize what most of the people presented in this book had in common:

1. They were all very driven in the pursuit of their "dream." From Elon Musk to Malala, and from William Kamkwamba to Ayah Bdeir, each of these people demonstrated "grit," which is the single quality that no one can teach you. They were determined to accomplish their goals, because they were convinced of the right view these goals represented. They found encouragement in the most ingenious ways, to reach the next level of their performance. Many of them came from extremely humble beginnings, but they did not allow their initial misery to keep them back. On the contrary, they used it as the wind beneath their wings! If they could do it, you can!

2. They were predominantly people from poor beginnings (as just mentioned). This is worth bringing up as a separate point, because there is a deeper intention behind their selection. Very few of the people discussed in this book were born under privileged circumstances. While some may have had a fairly comfortable life financially, none of them was excessively affluent to start with. This enhances the chance for you, the reader, to identify with them. There are no excuses to sit on the sideline and complain, because this book is filled with role models who dared to get up and go, and it led them way further than they ever dreamed they would be. If they could do it, you can!

3. They believed in education. Especially the younger individuals described made sure they obtained a college education, knowing that they would only be able to convince later generations to work on themselves if they could demonstrate that they had done the same. So, they worked hard, not only at the projects that made them well-known but also on their personal development, knowing that life is capricious and that circumstances may change any day. Yet, with a solid education, you have more options than just the one you currently deal with. An educated mind is able to see and

understand things that others have not learned to analyze. If they could do it, you can!

4. They did not feel that any demographic aspect should be a hurdle in their progress. We discussed men and women, younger and older people, and financially secure and dirt-poor people in this book: the diversity speaks for itself. What this is aimed to help you understand is that it is never too late to instigate a change in your life. It is never too late to start doing the right thing, to start engaging in right view, right intention, right speech, right action, right livelihood, right effort, right mindfulness, and right concentration. If they could do it, you can!

5. They did not accomplish their goals overnight. So many people get disheartened when their initiatives don't take off right away. At the first setback, they want to throw the towel in the ring and move on to another plan. Yet, while moving on to other plans is also part of life, you will not succeed if you don't persevere. Many people ask me, how do you know you should be holding on to something you are engaged in? The answer is simple: you are your best advisor. No one else can tell you when the right time is to give up. But as long as you feel passionate about something, and realize that there is a need to have it done, you should try to pursue it, no matter what others will say. If Wangari Maathai had listened to all the people who were criticizing her Greenbelt Movement efforts, she would not have won the Nobel Peace Prize. If Millard Fuller had become discouraged from all the people who would laugh at him when he said he was going to build homes for the poor without money, we would not have Habitat for Humanity today. If Howard Schultz had listened to all the people who undoubtedly told him that investing in the coffee store idea in America was going to be a disaster, we would not have Starbucks Coffee today. If Muhammad Yunus would have listened to the conventional banks, when they told him he should not trust poor people, because they were unable to do business, we would have never had micro-lending in the world. And we can go on with this line of reasoning ad infinitum. But here's the message: they did not allow others to discourage them. If they could do it, you can!

The Role of Kindness

A critical common point to bring up separately here is kindness: most of the people described in this book were driven by a deep-rooted kindness toward their actions. They were not driven by selfishness, even though some of them became very rich from their actions. Yet, their main drive was always to either establish something that they considered needed in their community, or correct a wrong in their society, or take something right to the next level.

I recently saw a quote that stated, "You will never regret being kind." Right beneath the quote, there were some interesting responses. One responder felt that you can get punished for being "wrongly kind," and another underscored this by reflecting on a bitter divorce, which she allotted to misplaced kindness on her end.

I believe that we could all come up with examples of kindness gone wrong according to our perception. You have probably also heard of the statement "No good deed goes unpunished." It is easy to attribute any disappointment that comes from interacting with another living being as abused kindness.

Yet, I think the problem lies in the *expectation* we have regarding our kindness: this is what causes more disappointment than anything else. All too often, we expect reciprocity from the one to whom we have been kind. In other words, if I have been kind to you, then you should be kind to me in return. And while that would be nice, of course, there is just as little guarantee for that to happen, as there is in the promise that we'll see another day.

What we often forget to consider is the following:

1. Kindness is an act onto itself. It should be deliberate, but not calculative, so it should not be tied to expectations.
2. The reward for our kindness comes from unexpected places, at unexpected times, and in unexpected forms. When we least expect it, we will receive some kind of blessing. The stories of the individuals described in this book abundantly attest to that.

It is interesting, however, that few of us wonder, when we are on the receiving end of life's kindnesses, what we did to deserve those. We just accept them and, if we're religious, we thank the lord or existence, but then we move on.

A more rational way of considering kindness is as a humane duty: an unwritten rule for valuable and gratifying existence. The gratification starts when we stop expecting kindness in return from those to whom we have been kind. There is no wrongful kindness. Kindness is kind onto itself. It's a virtue, and the world can use much more of it.

There is a broader scope we should consider when thinking about kindness: wherever we can lend a helping hand, that's where we should give it. It's common knowledge, and yet, so hard to do on a consistent basis. We're all so busy with getting ahead. Nothing wrong with that, as long as we keep in mind that, wherever we can, we should be kind—without expectations—and refrain from harming others, and that doesn't only pertain to human beings…

This brings to mind a Zen story about two monks and a scorpion. The two monks were walking in the rain and saw a scorpion almost drowning in a water bowl. One of the monks reached into the bowl to save the scorpion, but it painfully stung him every time he tried. After witnessing this several times, the other monk asked his friend why he kept trying to save the stinging creature. As he finally picked up a leaf and released the scorpion that way, the monk smilingly said, "To sting is the scorpion's nature. To save is mine. My kindness and compassion are not discouraged that easily".[1]

Whether in professional, social, or private environments, we will encounter both, reciprocated and negligent responses to our kindness. The best way to deal with any of these circumstances is to understand that no one owes us anything and that we will receive our share of kindness at the right time. No sooner, no later.

Connecting Heart and Mind

We are leaders by birth. Each and every one of us, currently alive. We are leaders by the virtue of being the one who got conceived, and made it all the way to the here and now.

We are filled with a blend of seemingly contradictory qualities, such as fighting spirit and the desire to live in peace, the ability to be driven yet patient, the urge to compete yet embrace, etc.

We use these qualities at moments we deem appropriate. The insight and sensitivity to apply the proper skill at the proper moment is an example of our leadership.

As leaders, we find our path through the unknown territory that is life. Sometimes we feel comfortable and at other times insecure. It's part of our growth.

Every moment, day, week, month, or year in our life provides us with jewels that are building blocks toward the leader we become. Whether windfalls or setbacks, the purpose always becomes clear in hindsight: everything is an element of construction toward our leadership.

---

[1] Monk and Scorpion. Retrieved from http://buddhistreflections.blogspot.com/2011/01/monk-and-scorpion.html

The process of leadership development doesn't end during our lifetime. It continues till the day we move on from this stage of being. And this entire process is captured as a "dash" once our last breath has been uttered.

The best we can do is to remain mindful as often as possible and learn to see every experience as an opportunity to cultivate the leader in us. Some critical, heart-mind connecting skills to accrue in the process:

- *Perseverance*
  Understand that nothing comes from giving up without trying repeatedly. Your greatest achievements are usually those that require incessant effort and going an extra mile long after others have given up.
- *Courage*
  Taking initiatives is not an easy task. You will find yourself fearful and doubtful of many efforts. Yet, little can be achieved if you are lethargic. If you can work up the courage to act, you will find yourself looking back with a sense of fulfillment. Leading means daring.
- *Encouragement*
  As you grow in life, you'll find that there is tremendous intrinsic fulfillment in lending a helping hand (or listening ear) to others. Witnessing their growth and seeing them succeed will provide a lasting sense of meaning to your life.
- *Collaboration*
  We are not islands but interconnected particles that perform best when we involve others in our efforts. I find that this element, while understood, is one we continuously have to polish some more, especially if we have the tendency to do things on our own.
- *Compassion*
  Many people consider compassion unbefitting in leadership, but it turns out that trying to understand others is a very useful and rewarding tool to increased trust and collaboration, as long as you handle your compassion with care.
- *Ambition*
  While ambition is a quality that needs to be monitored with care, it remains of high use in taking the lead and making a success of it. Having a decent dosage of ambition inside can determine the difference between being a trendsetter or a follower of trends.

Infuse these behavioral ingredients in your daily practices, and you may proudly label yourself an awakened leader.

Understanding the Here and Now

This Moment

This moment is precious
Because I'm in the mood
To use it for nothing
Which is a scarce good
In these crowded days
Where three jobs are accrued
For the price of one

This moment is precious
because I use it to respect
the breath that drives me –
the one I rarely detect
as I go – day by day
while it keeps me intact
and gets my work done

This moment is precious
so I name it "Peace"
because of what it brings:
a sense of calm and ease
even though I know that
this, too, will soon cease
for life goes on

This moment is precious
because it will not last
soon enough it will be
a fragment of the past
and I will wonder
why it went so fast
                    ~Joan Marques

Leading your life (and leading other people) can be a challenge, especially on days that you are less cheerful. No matter how upbeat you are by nature, there are days that you feel as if there is a cloud hanging over your head, and it just doesn't want to be shaken off. Here are five "right" thoughts that could make you feel better in almost any situation:

1. *Wherever I am at the moment, is where I am supposed to be.*
   Much of your discontentment arises from a sense of anxiety that you made a wrong move and are trapped in a situation that you should exit. While it is definitely healthy to look ahead and work on improving your circumstances, it is equally important to know that every experience is valuable and that this stage, regardless of how dull, irritable, or dreadful it may seem at times, fulfills a purpose in your life. When least expected, you will realize what the value was of experiencing this moment.

2. *Many of my old troubles have been resolved, so whatever bothers me today shall pass as well.*
   In moments of doubt, it can be useful to reflect on past misfortunes, not because you choose to wallow in them, but because they could be instrumental in stirring your understanding and awareness that everything is a passing stage. Former troubles are the best confirmations of this piece of reality and can create a sense of relief, as well as kindle renewed energy toward future improvement.

3. *I have no need to envy anyone because I don't know the troubles under the surface of their glamor, nor would I want to.*
   One of the biggest letdowns is the habit of comparing yourself to others. There will always be someone with a better paid job, more popularity, a nicer car, a more expensive outfit, or better looks. Should this be a reason to feel sorry for yourself? Absolutely not! After all, we all bear our own blessings and troubles. Just remember the old adage that if everyone could throw their troubles on a pile and choose those of others, they would most likely take their own bag of troubles home again.

4. *My life is an inspiration to at least one other person, even if (s)he remains anonymous.*
   You may be down on yourself today, but in the course of your lifetime, you have surely touched the heart of someone else. Whether or not that person ever stepped forward to share that with you doesn't matter. But such is the beauty of life: we interact, share, and absorb. And just as you have learned from others, they have learned from you as well.

5. *I am aware of my circumstances today, and I can decide at any time to start writing my story for tomorrow.*
   You are the only one who can place the first step toward any change in your circumstances. All it takes is awareness. If you can shake off self-pity, lethargy, and fear, you can start thinking and exploring new directions in your life. Nothing stays the same forever. Today is just as fleeting as yesterday was. So, start writing your future. Now is a great time!

Dealing with Regrets

There is a beautiful song by Adele, titled "Million Years Ago." In this song, to which I invite you to listen through any of the media outlets, the singer bewails her life, as it seemed to have slipped through her fingers, filling her with regret about the many opportunities she failed to cease and the many blunders she made. She laments, in an emotionally laden way, that she realizes she is not the only one with feelings of being a failure for not having achieved what she thought she should: a truly beautiful song that gives rise to deep emotions and even deeper thought. And here's my thought:

> We can, indeed, regret the many missed chances in our lives, and dwell on our numerous disappointments – many of us do just that – but doing so only makes today's reality rather gloomy. There is another side – there always is – and in this case, it is the choice we have to look at all our experiences, the highs and lows, the victories and the defeats, the elations and the devastations, and consider the increased wisdom, sensitivity, and resilience they brought us today. There's nothing new about the assertion that we are mostly the product of our past choices, since the person we are at this moment has only come this far *because* of all the things that went right and wrong in the past.

> That being said, I also realize that it is not easy to step over a dreadful experience. Sometimes we mentally beat ourselves for years for making what we may consider one of the biggest blunders in our lives. However, when we finally achieve the next windfall, we promptly forget to look back and realize that our past troubles were instrumental in preparing us for this glorious moment. Along the same lines, many of us seem to have a tendency to engage in self-deprecation by downplaying our accomplishments. I was just communicating with a colleague, who, in the not-so-far past, had held a prestigious leadership position in a highly respected organization, and I was pointing out to her what a great accomplishment this was… upon which she responded that it all did not mean anything, because she only got the position due to someone else stepping down. I felt compelled to invite my dear colleague to review the situation from another angle: the time had arrived for her to take over the reins of this organization, which was why the other person had to step down!

> I am not promoting arrogance here. Quite the contrary! What I am promoting is insight and gratitude for all that comes on our path: the things that seem wonderful and those that look meaningless, or even sour. In the end, they will all serve a purpose, even if we cannot see—or appreciate—that purpose today.

Oh I agree that we all encounter situations that make us mad, sad, disappointed, or even devastated. Thinking back, I cannot help but recall the old song, "My Way," with the famous wording, "Regrets? I've had a few. But then again, too few to mention." As I mature in life, I find myself having fewer rather than more regrets, because I have learned to see the reason behind, and the value of, every situation I once regretted.

None of us reaches maturity without a few feathers that have been plucked away from our cap. However, if we open ourselves to the mindset that even the most regrettable moments happen for a reason, we can learn to cope better with them, and if we evaluate ourselves today, we may find that some new, even more colorful feathers have been added to that same cap.

So, here's my final note:

Never consider any defeat an endpoint: there's always something better coming up.

Open your mind for opportunities—don't let tunnel vision drain your mental cup.

Reap the benefits of life's free lessons: every experience represents one.
Energize yourself when things are tough. Only you can get that done.
Give more than you take. You will be rewarded in the end.
Realize that there are ups and downs to every life well-spent.
Engage in positive self-dialogues: the best boosts come from within.
Trust your inner compass: it's that only responsible way to win.
Stop those negative emotions: this is a great moment to begin!

Maintaining the Right Intentions

As leaders in our life (and of others), it's also important to know that every behavior can serve as an advantage or a pitfall, depending on the intensity we invest in it. Perseverance, usually considered a strong quality, could evolve into annoying persistence long after the sense of achieving our goal has faded. The desire to ensure growth and profitability in our performance could morph into selfish greed; the aim to gain prominence may turn into damaging pride; the motivation about achieving a goal could degenerate into an excessive end-focus; the urge to realize a potentially noble initiative may lead to rationalization of unacceptable acts; and the quality of being patient, tolerant, or understanding may dilute into apathy.

Let's briefly review some of the pitfalls that can cause leaders to lose sight of their moral path and fall prey to some of the most common downsides of performance orientation.

Greed

When we stand at the bottom of the career ladder, we are always filled with good intentions. In my many years as a facilitator of seminars for upcoming business leaders, I have yet to meet one that said (s)he would become a greedy, ruthless executive. Greed grows on us when we fail to closely monitor our motives. It is a notorious by-product of the desire to be a winner. Corporate leaders, but also those with fighting spirit in different settings, can relate to this: as you fight your way to the top, you focus so much on your own victory that you may become blind to the needs of others and ignorant to the way you are perceived. By the time you realize what happened, you may find yourself too deeply anchored in the behavior of selfish gaining to find a way out.

Pride

Pride can be a downside of many factors. It can surface when a leader works on his or her self-confidence, and does such a good job at it, that (s)he ultimately thinks (s)he has all the answers. This type of pride is frequently labeled as "arrogance." Pride can also manifest itself in the sense of not wanting to lose face. Some leaders have so much trouble admitting that they were wrong and that they would rather manipulate data, contaminate people, and risk valuable relationships, only to prove their right. Pride is an easy gateway to becoming so self-indulged that one may start thinking that (s)he stands above the law and therefore may engage in acts that are unacceptable for others.

Excessive End-Focus

This moral flaw has the best chance of surfacing when critical and pressing goals need to be met. In such circumstances it is easy to fall prey to the mindset that achieving the numbers justifies everything, even a few unethical acts. This, then, is when we can see leaders betraying their employees' psychological contracts by continuously demanding more output from them without giving any additional rewards; callously disregarding employees' work-life balance for the sake of the meeting or exceeding deadlines; and even shipping substandard or damaged products in order to justify quota.

Rationalization

This is yet another quality that sounds really good, but can also have its dark sides. In dire times, leaders can begin to rationalize why engaging in less than rosy practices could be justified. For years, now, I have presented business students a dilemma that boils down to the following: should you use illegally acquired data from a competitor to win a bidding or forego the opportunity and risk going out of business? So far, the responses have been even: half of the participants stated that they would not use the data, as it would be blatantly immoral, and half came up with all sorts of rationalizations as to why they would use the information, even though they knew it was unethical. Some of the most common rationalizations of immoral acts are everyone does it, this is my fair right in an unfair world, or it's part of my responsibility.

Apathy

Knowing that others are engaging in something immoral and not doing anything about it, even if you can, is as immoral as being fully involved. Apathy is the ugly side of acceptance, but while acceptance is usually a positive quality, we can push it too far, just as we could any other good quality, and become complacent about the status quo, even if it's an undesirable one. Being apathetic is inexcusable in leadership, because leaders are supposed to know what is going on in their environments.

Keeping track of the just discussed moral pitfalls may keep us more on our leadership toes and assist us in becoming the role models we aspire to be for upcoming generations.

Seize Your Opportunities

The days in which we currently live are challenging in many ways: change happens at a continuous and dazzling speed, professions on which society was built for the longest time are disappearing, the job market is incessantly shifting with many opportunities moving to other parts of the world, and learning in itself has never been a more ambiguous process, because the future is unpredictable, so you can't possibly know what you are really preparing yourself for.

And yet, these are days of great opportunities. Whatever you want to know is basically at your fingertips. Those of us who are older remember the pre-Internet days, when knowledge had to be obtained from libraries, news programs, or expensive encyclopedias. It was therefore limited to time, accessibility, and means. Nothing was as instantaneous as it is today. It took quite some effort to get to the source of any piece of information needed. The ease with which we can currently access global databases and news sources or simply obtain answers to general—or specific—questions is astounding, even though it has become the new "normal," making very few people reflect on the blessing captured in this status quo.

If you have any kind of talent, you don't need a whole lot of funds or connections with powerful people to display what you can: the social networks offer plentiful opportunities to share your skills, and many of today's successes found their initial push through the net.

Being an introvert is no longer a barrier to meeting people and establishing rewarding connections. Great friendships and wonderful long-term relationships—even marriages—were established and cultivated through the same medium that was responsible for the two previously mentioned advantages, the Internet.

Borders are no longer barriers, because people now continuously communicate with one another through numerous venues at thousands of miles' distance as if they were sitting right beside each other. Costs are also a disappearing barrier, because internet and telephone connections have seen their most expensive days. We are heading toward a world without borders, and with that, one with greater mutual acceptance and understanding.

Dreaming has never been as attractive as it is today, because the chance to realize your dreams has never been so abundantly present. So, why would the turnaround of people's lives be limited to unknown individuals? More than ever, we all have it in our hands to determine who and what we want to be.

With knowledge, relationships, insights, and exploratory tools within arms' reach, we really have little or no excuse to be left behind. The only thing we need from ourselves is willpower and courage. Those qualities are not for sale and cannot be taught per se. But they can be mustered and cultivated, because we all have them in our system.

With all the opportunities within reach, staying behind has practically become a non-option. So, what are your plans?

Final Note

The world is a fascinating, aggravating, heartwarming, daunting, hope-giving, shattering, touching place. Ambivalent, mesmerizing, unpredictable. I wonder if anyone ever tried to assess the ratio between good and bad things happening on a daily basis. I guess not, because it would be practically impossible with so many occurrences not being recorded or simply not observed. But regardless of how we choose to perceive our worldly habitat at the moment, it remains what it is: the place where the boat of our life takes off and sails until it sinks. And this is the point that has resurfaced in my mind lately. I read this quote by Shunryu Suzuki "Life is like stepping onto a boat which is about to sail out to sea and sink." It's a pretty gloomy but very true statement. We all step into our little boat at birth and sail in it until that unknown day when we will go down. There's nothing surer than that.

And yet, we get caught in a mental maze that propels and compels us into actions that seem so important at the moment, but that will indubitably evaporate somewhere in the future, because everything comes and goes. No exceptions there either. Still, we cannot allow this ominous thought get a hold of us, because sitting by the wayside is simply not an option. Performance is the motto, and to be honest, without that, living would be a dull affair. So, I guess the secret to fulfillment in this challenging, unknown journey of ours is to discover our personal balance and find that happy medium between achieving and unwinding, sprinting and straggling, and striving and resting.

It's so easy to get carried away by the daily turbulences and suffer sleepless nights in order to satisfy our ambition, but the thought of this little boat that sails until it sinks can be a marvelous internal wake-up call to calm us down when we try to surpass ourselves.

So, here are three thoughts to consider:

1. Don't compare. When others get more recognition for their actions, you could consider their actions as a motivator for your own, but you should never try to do exactly what they do. They are different, and so is their boat.
2. Don't lose sight of the big picture. In the larger scheme of things, your actions, although important, are a small part in the mosaic of life. Don't over- or underestimate yourself. Do what you can and do it well, but make sure you have fun while doing it, and don't neglect your loved ones, your health, and your happiness.
3. Keep your COURAGE intact:

   Choice: there are multiple options to (almost) everything.
   Open-mindedness: don't shut unconventional opportunities out.
   Usefulness: celebrate everything you encounter. It'll be useful one day.
   Reality-check: know that what you see is not necessarily what others see.
   Attitude: Look at life from the bright side, and never stay down long.
   Genius: Keep that spark of unbridled intelligence in you alive.
   Education: Stay open to learning.

Happy sailing!

A Lost Day

Lost is the day in which you have not found fulfillment in any area:
work, private, or social.

Lost is the day in which you have not found a reason to smile:
not about others, and not about yourself.

Lost is the day in which you have not been of any service:
neither to others, nor to yourself.

Lost is the day in which you have not shared
some love with another living creature.

Lost is the day in which you did not dedicate
one positive thought to yourself.

Lost is the day in which your laziness
prevented you to be constructive.

Lost is the day in which you allowed
the setbacks and failures of the world to get the best of you.

Lost is the day in which you allowed
your jealousy to conquer your compassion.

Lost is the day in which you undertook
any act with a devious intention.

Lost is the day in which your mind
prevailed your heart.

Lost is the day in which you allowed
material gain to determine your decisions.

Lost is the day in which you sought out
a prey among the vulnerable.

Lost is the day in which you
discarded empathy.

Lost is the day in which you preferred ignorance,
through discrimination of any kind, to embracement of equality.

Lost is the day in which you got lost in backbiting
and any other kind of meanness directed toward another.

Lost is the day in which you failed to recognize
the lesson in even the most dreadful experience.

Lost is the day in which you ignored
the voice of your intuition.

Lost is the day in which you did not prioritize
the ones you love over material gain.

Lost is the day in which you
lowered yourself to hypocrisy.

Lost is the day in which you deliberately
brought pain upon another living creature.

Lost is the day in which you
allowed hope to get lost.

Lost is the day in which you
forgot where you came from.

Lost is the day in which you
forget where you're going.

Lost is the day in which you allowed an estrangement
between your mind, your body, and your soul.

Lost is the day in which
you were not creative.

Lost is the day in which you lost
the connection with the source within...

~Joan Marques

CPSIA information can be obtained
at www.ICGtesting.com
Printed in the USA
LVHW010029150819
627732LV00002B/12/P